building small small groups

in the Christian community.

John Mallison
(and a small group)

No. 1 in the Abridged Small Group Series

Dedication

To the inter-generational small group
from which I receive my greatest support,
and whose co-leader is my wife, June.
The other five active members being
Graham, Paul, Andrew, Lynelle and Matthew.

ISBN 0 85421 905 6

First published by Renewal Publications, Box 130, West Ryde, N.S.W. 2114, Australia
First English edition in this format 1981. Scripture Union, 130 City Road, London EC1V 2NJ
Reprinted 1981, 1983

Printed in England by Scripture Union. ,

Scripture Union
130 City Road, London EC1V 2NJ.

Foreword

This book is the first of two which replace the four books of the original Small Group Book Series. It presents the theoretical material on Christian small groups. The second book "Creative Ideas for Small Groups in the Christian Community" contains practical procedures for use in small groups. Much of the material in this book is the outcome of my own parish ministry and overseas experiences and has been refined in the workshop atmosphere of the small group leadership training courses I have conducted throughout Australia and in other countries.

I am grateful to the leaders and members of the small groups in my parishes and to every course participant who has helped me in this work.

The original books met with an excellent response and after the second edition it was decided to publish this abridged and revised series to make them more widely available. The bulk of the original material is retained. I am grateful to a number of Christian educators and parish leaders who helped in the selection of the material which they found to be most helpful.

Where local churches are bearing a significant witness or where there is dynamic Christian life it is likely that small groups are the heartbeat of that new life. The small group is the most flexible and versatile structure we have within the Christian church. It can be adapted to almost any situation to meet a wide variety of needs. It is my hope that all who read this book will catch the vision of the possibilities of small groups for bringing renewal to the Christian community and gain some understanding of how to commence and maintain these life giving cells.

I wish to acknowledge the help of a number of people in the preparation of the original books. Wendy Cowling for her mammoth task in undertaking the editorial and production work and for her wise and patient counsel; Graham Beattie, Helen Chapman, Gordon Dicker, Brenda Fowler, Athol Gill, Elva Harris, Ross Kingham, David Manton, Doug Parker, John Paton, Margaret Tarbotton, Janet Wade and others who helped with the revision and expansion of the original material, wrote specialized contributions, sent in reports of their work or advised me in a variety of ways. My thanks to June Bosenquet for her editorial work and advice with this new series.

This book has been made possible by the support of the Department of Christian Education, of the Congregational, Methodist and Presbyterian Churches, Sydney, and since the union of the three churches, the Board of Education. The kindness and co-operation of many people is also gratefully acknowledged.

My warm appreciation also to Gloster Udy for his affirmation and counsel in connection with my first major involvement in small groups at Port Kembla which laid the foundation of my contribution to the small group movement.

My grateful thanks to my wife June for her support and encouragement.

We offer this book in love to all those who read it and seek to apply it.

John Mallison

Acknowledgements

All rights to this series are claimed by the author and publishers. A great deal of material in the small group movement is becoming common domain; ideas have originated in one place and have been varied, changed, or used as a basis in others. We are indebted to such work. A small amount of material in this series has been adapted or copied from roneoed sheets, received from a variety of sources and on which there was no indication of copyright.

We are indebted too for the inspiration of many pioneers in this field — to Keith Miller, Lyman Coleman, Samuel Shoemaker, Bruce Larson and others who have opened up the exploration of new concepts and new areas for the Church today.

We acknowledge with thanks Zondervan for permission to quote from Lawrence A. Richards' *A New Face for the Church*; Louis Evans Jnr, for permission to reproduce a suggested outline for a covenant agreement, which first appeared in *Faith at Work*; John Kleinig and ANZEA for permission to quote from *The Group*.

The photographs are by Scripture Union & the author

Cover design by Liz Norman-Clarke

Contributors:

Gordon Dicker is a Uniting Church minister and a member of the staff of the United Theological College, Sydney.

Graeme Beattie is a Uniting Church minister in Sydney. Prior to entering the ministry he was working in business management.

Ross Kingham is a Uniting Church minister in Canberra.

Athol Gill is Principal of Whitley College, Melbourne.

Contents

1 Small Groups within the Christian Church

"The Gospel must be brought back to where people live, in simple forms, and in terms of small and manageable fellowships."

Stephen Neill.

"I began my revolution with eighty-two men. If I had to do it again I would do it with ten or fifteen men and absolute faith. It does not matter how small you are, providing you have faith and a plan of action."

Fidel Castro.

The Small Group is the basic building block of the life of the local congregation and is fundamental to the development of individual and corporate Christian life-style. This is my judgement after reflection on 17 years in a parish situation during which we built much of the local church life and witness upon small groups. It has been deepened and confirmed by my personal involvement in a variety of small groups outside the local church and my observations of small groups in Australia and overseas. The many helpful books and articles which have appeared on the subject only support this conviction.

The small group movement has always been a significant force for renewal in the Christian church but its place is being re-discovered again in our time. However, they are not limited to the church — in our contemporary society small groups have also become a way of life in the last two or three decades. The behavioural sciences are assigning numerous roles to face-to-face groups. Today group training is seen as a basic tool in business and management, and in working with organizations of all kinds. Therapy groups are used to help those with personality problems or serious mental illness. Group counselling is often used with troubled families, as well as with alcoholics, drug addicts, and weight watchers.

Of course the "small group movement" has been perverted, as are all movements. Some so-called "sensitivity groups" have engaged in all sorts of excesses. But the excesses shouldn't blind us to the discovered facts about human nature and our need for one another.

When we talk about **small** group structures, "small" suggests a size which permits and encourages face-to-face relationships. It is not so large that any will be cut off from deeply and personally sharing themselves with others, and in turn receiving them. How large is this? Some research in group dynamics suggests that five may be the optimum number. But often groups of eight or twelve are suggested for church fellowship groups, and this range seems to have many advantages.

Simply throwing eight or twelve Christians together does not make them a group. Nor will it, in itself, ensure that they will develop life. Members, may, over a span of many meetings, remain strangers who share nothing more significant than what each thinks the others want to hear. A small group which functions as the church needs to develop group life. Without initial guidance and help, or without an understanding of how the group can become the church of its members, a small group may move far off course.

Why a small group?

Many convincing arguments are put forward by the behavioural sciences to support the important role of small groups in society today. However I want to briefly advance some theological reasons for the place of small groups in the Christian community. Our understanding of Christian group dynamics arises out of our commitment to Christ and its implications for our life together.

Small groups are essential **because of the quality of life we seek.** A basic reason for the small group is the need to know others intimately in order to become the church. The group life of a local congregation should be characterized by its experience of oneness in Christ. This involves a gathering together of the disciples of Christ, a shared sense of identity as a body and a deep commitment to and love for each other. It is obvious that this quality of life is found in few local congregations today! *"By this all men will know that you are my disciples, if you have love for one another."* Only a minority of Christian congregations could be seen to be fulfilling this Royal Law of our Lord.

This distinguishing mark of true Christian fellowship will most likely not be rediscovered in large meetings where the participants seldom see each other during the week. For in such situations we do not truly **know** each other. We cannot truly **love,** because we are not able to be involved in each other's lives. In large congregations most must remain strangers. Few have opportunity to share themselves or feel free to be truly honest.

Lawrence Richards writes:

"To learn to trust, and to become trustworthy — to learn to love, and to become loving — we must become deeply involved in the lives of others, to whom we commit ourselves in Christ. To develop this kind of relationship we need to share ourselves with others, and they need to share themselves with us. All of this demands time. More than this, it requires a face-to-face relationship. A relationship we can have only with a few others at one time. And thus a church is forced to move to a small group structure."[1]

Another reason lies in **the nature of the spiritual growth we seek** says Richards. Spiritual growth is certainly concerned with change in ideas and in belief systems. But rightly understood, it is essentially concerned with character change — transformation of attitudes, of values, of personality, and these are socially anchored. They are learned through associating with others. They cannot be developed in isolation. For this new set of attitudes, values and behaviour the Christian disciple needs a social anchor. He needs a viable, authentic, supportive, accepting group in which the Word of God is studied and lived out by its members, individually and collectively.

Richards in his discussion of such change in people, quotes from the *Handbook of Small Group Research* by A. Paul Hore (p. 287) "A whole series of studies shows that if one wishes to change attitudes and the subsequent behaviour of a group, discussion and decision where all members participate as directly as possible tends to be more effective than 'enlightenment' or 'persuasion' by the lecture method."

Lawrence Richards goes on to say, "In giving this vital role to the small group I am not in the least suggesting we diminish the role of Scripture. Rather we place Scripture as central to the life of the small group, as will be developed later. I do point out, however, that our normal method of teaching God's Word (by sermon) has both communication limitations and also serious limitations on life-impact. Certainly I do not deny that the Holy Spirit uses the preached

9

Word. I only insist that He is much freer to use the Word in a small group where it is studied and discussed together, and that this is one of God's purposes in creating the church."

Small groups play an important role **because God calls us to live out our Christian life in community,** not simply as independent individuals. John Kleinig makes this point in his book *The Group — Its Nature and Role*

> "It is as individuals that we enter into a permament relationship with Christ . . . this personal relationship is lived out in fellowship with others; *all of us are the parts of one body' (Eph. 4:25 NEB)*. Group membership is not an optional extra for God's people. When a person responds in faith to Jesus Christ he is brought into relationship with others of God's people in that locality — he becomes a group member. This group, community, congregation or assembly of God's people, as it is conceived in the Old and New Testaments is thus not viewed simply as a sociological phenomenon, for it is thought of primarily in terms of God's call."[2]

We are called into a special relationship with each other with privileges and responsibilities *(Galatians 6:10, 1 Corinthians 16:1; Colossians 3:12-17)*. Mutual dependence and influence upon, and respect for each other are required of those in "the Body of Christ". And each small group is seen by Paul as being "the Body of Christ". The writer of the Epistle to the Hebrews enjoins each believer to not avoid these opportunities for Christian nurture and worship.

> "—and let us think of one another and how we can encourage each other to love and do good deeds. And let us not hold aloof from our church meetings, as some do. Let us do all we can to help one another's faith, and this the more earnestly as we see the final day drawing nearer
> *(Hebrews 10:24, 25, J. B. Phillips)*.

We are not saved in an isolated and individualistic fashion — but salvation brings us into close relationship with each other.

A further reason why we should meet in small groups is **because of the nature of the ministry which every Chris-** Ministry of believers tian disciple is called to exercise. When the New Testament speaks of ministry in a local church, it is a ministry of all believers to each other. In the passage quoted above from Hebrews chapter 10, the exhortation is not to avoid gathering together because we have a responsibility to minister to each other. When "two or three" or more disciples are gathered Christ is there ministering through each to the other encouraging one another's faith. Each is potentially a minister as well as one who also must be prepared to be ministered to by others in the group. Each is potentially a stimulator of the faith of the others, as well as a learner. Certainly in Ephesians four ministers seem to be appointed to fulfil special roles but these gifted people served in such a way "that Christians might be properly equipped for **their** ministry."

In such passages as 1 Peter 4:9f; 1 Corinthians chs. 12 to 14 (12:4 to 31, 14:26); Romans 12:4-8, the key features of ministry are that: each Christian disciple has a gift, a special ability from God. There are varied abilities and ministries. These abilities are to be used for "the common good" of the group to which we belong.

Small groups are essential in the life of the church, providing situations in which this mutuality of ministry can take place. Only a small number can minister in a large gathering and then only in a fairly superficial manner to each individual in that crowd. The majority are denied an opportunity to exercise their ministry to the gathered church. For all these reasons, then, the small group is vital to the church facing renewal. In no other way can we move so quickly toward becoming the church. In no other situation can the functions of the church be so fully carried out. In no other context can the Word of God be communicated with so much impact on lives. The church today, as the church of the New Testament, needs the "church in the house". We need the small group.

**Small Groups
are not new**

Small groups are not new to the Christian church. The groups which are bringing renewal to the church today have long roots in the past which go beyond Christ to the background which the Jewish faith gives to Christianity. Even in the ancient Jewish church there were small societies of friends who met on the Sabbath eve for supper and prayer. Such groups were called *"chaburah"*.

Jesus and His disciples, most probably, formed such a

company which differed from others only in the exceptionally close bond of love and mutual commitment that drew them to their leader, and the independent attitude of Jesus toward accepted religious authorities.

Mark records **"and he appointed twelve, to be with him,** and **to be sent out** to **preach** and **have authority** to cast out demons *(3:14, 15)*. In the company of a small close group, Jesus revealed Himself most fully. Peter, James and John were present at His Transfiguration. The twelve shared the Last Supper. The three were with Him again in Gethsemane.

Our Lord concentrated on the training of twelve men of no conspicuous ability. With a whole world to save He spent most of His ministry, it would seem, in private with this little group. He set out to teach those men to love one another and to pass on the good news of God's love to others. One cannot miss the significance of the twelve, in searching for ways to vitalize the Church of our day.

The early church followed the model the Lord gave to them. At Pentecost a group was gathered in prayer. Early records give the vivid description of the church, *"They continued steadily learning the teaching of the apostles, and joined in their fellowship, in the breaking of bread, and in prayer" (Acts 2:42) ". . . . they broke bread together in their homes, sharing meals with simple joy" (Acts 2:46).*

In its infancy the church **was** these small groups who gathered to share with one another the intimate things the Holy Spirit worked within their lives.

> "In New Testament times to be a Christian was to belong to a fellowship of believers who had big things to accomplish and needed one another's support to get them done. But more than this they needed the common life centered in Christ. They banded together to talk about him, to listen to his Spirit speak to them, to read from the Scripture, to ponder the letters of their leaders, and to eat together the bread of communion at his table. He said he would come when two or three of them gathered together in his name. They believed his promise and felt his Presence."[3]

In the intervening history of the church new spiritual life has been marked by the emergence of small groups. In the middle ages amidst a church which had grown fat and short of breath through prosperity and muscle-bound by over-organization, dynamic Christians such as St. Francis of Assisi gathered in small groups for prayer and study, training and service. They kept a flame burning amidst the darkness of a decaying ecclesiasticism. Various sections of the Anabaptist movement in Europe formed dynamic house-centred groups. The Hutterites in Moravia, Southern Germany, lived out a New Testament-styled community life which had a far-reaching impact. George Fox brought fresh power to the church through the clusters of small groups which became known as the Religious Society of Friends.

The small group in Methodism

Methodism actually began with a small *"koinonia"* group comprising just four students at Oxford University. They contracted with each other to study the Scriptures, live a Christian lifestyle, witness verbally and undertake social concern both collectively and individually. The special characteristic of the Wesleyan Revival in the eighteenth century was the small "class meeting". Here the socially elite and the wretched and the outcast found hope. Social barriers were broken down within these small groups of ten to twelve members and a deep sense of unity within diversity resulted. They became structures of hope in a decaying society which hung on the brink of a revolution. Lives were transformed and a spiritual awakening brought to England and beyond.

The beginning of the Class Meeting is due to a layman, Captain Foy by name. It really arose from Wesley's desire to raise the necessary finance to pay off the debt on a room built in 1739 near the Horsefair in Bristol. Foy suggested that every member of the Society give a penny a week till the debt was liquidated. He then offered to collect from eleven of the poorest members, and even went so far as to offer to pay the instalment of any of the group who found difficulty in meeting the liability. Wesley's fertile brain soon saw the value in this from the standpoint of spiritual oversight. He called the leaders of the classes together, and desired that they should make weekly inquiries as to the behaviour of each class member. More than a financial method had been discovered.

Soon meetings were held in the Bristol Room. Advice or reproof was given as need required, quarrels made up, misunderstandings removed, and after an hour or two, they concluded with prayer and thanksgiving. The meetings were open to all desiring spiritual help. At a quarterly gathering Wesley or one of his assistants gave tickets of membership to each. Wesley saw in this system of forming local societies, and their division into classes, a revival of primitive Christianity. In addition to the resemblance to early Christianity, Wesley had seen such classes working amongst the Moravians at Hernhutt, and later at Febler Lane, as well as at the Foundry.

The working of the plan required people who might well be called sub-pastors — in itself this was the establishment of a new ministry of the laity. Christians were held together, the lapsed were sought after and brought back and thus the company of the faithful was built up. Wesley made the widest use of the consecrated layman as class-leaders. These men and women were incomparably more influential in early Methodism than those who in more recent years have been known as 'local preachers'. Many of them were outstanding evangelists — though they seldom or never preached. They worked continuously inviting people to the classes and dealing personally with them until they "found" God and were seeking "perfect love" (i.e. trying to lead a Christ-like life.) The decline in the vitality of Methodism since the latter part of the 19th Century has been attributed to the withdrawal of the requirement that members regularly attend a class meeting for nurture and direction.

The revival of the small group

In the last two decades or more there has been taking place what Hobart Mowrer calls "a quiet revolution". Around the world one of the signs of hope in the Christian church has been the renewal being brought to individuals and Christian communities through the formation of small groups. Some are linked together through large movements such as the Faith at Work, Yokefellows, the Anglican Prayer Fellowship and the United Methodist's Koinonia Groups and Ten Brave Christians (or John Wesley's Experiment) in the U.S.A., or the world wide Charismatic fellowship and healing movements. Others are part of parish level networks of small groups. Many are isolated groups of people meeting out of a deep sense of need to take seriously the Lordship of Christ.

These small fellowships of renewal are to be found in factories and offices, schools and universities, city restaurants and suburban homes. They meet at a variety of times, some over breakfast or lunch. There are morning and afternoon groups, some gather in the evening and others over supper. Some meet well before dawn to avoid the distractions of the daily routine. Within the church and outside the church, men and women are exploring together the deep things of the Spirit and in many cases bringing a new influence to bear upon society.

The witness of ministers, leaders and participants in this new movement is most encouraging. As in the reports included in the chapter "Innovations in Small Groups", they testify that such groups have an amazing ministry to those who take them seriously. Homes and churches are changed, lives are transformed, a new sense of unity reached and a commitment to a world in need.

The testimony of Scripture, the record of history and the witness of our contemporaries makes that very clear; spiritual renewal does come to the church whenever a nucleus responds to Christ in depth and when they do this together in intimate fellowship. The Holy Spirit works with revolutionary power when small companies of Christians reach new levels of openness and expectation and respond to His inner promptings in obedience and faith. "If such groups will act as a kind of spearhead of awakening, strive constantly to be humble and teachable, and let the Holy Spirit be the Strategist that forms them all into 'an exceeding great army' under His leadership alone, there is literally no telling what might happen in our day."[4]

Not all small groups have been successful

Small groups in the Christian Church have not always had an impressive history. While many have been successful many have failed. There is no magic in the small group itself. On occasions I meet people who respond to my vision of the potential of small groups in the Christian Church with, "Oh, we tried them years ago and they didn't work." Small groups in the church have not always fulfilled the expectations of the participants because they have either not understood, or put into practice, certain basic principles which help to keep group life vital such as those dealt with in chapter 9. Even a limited understanding of group dynamics would have saved some groups from not achieving their purpose. Many groups in the church have not developed into real communities of care and concern because it was not in God's timing or because they were commenced with inferior motives.

Many have looked upon small groups as another gimmick to get the church back on the rails again, to prop up failing structures. Dietrich Bonhoeffer has described much of the conventional concept of discipleship in terms of what he calls "cheap grace". "Cheap grace" in small group life is Bible study without action, prayer without creativity, fellowship without care and concern, sharing without honesty, community without contracts. "Cheap grace' is grace without repentance, discipleship without the Cross, togetherness without a living ever-present Christ.

Spiritual renewal requires man's co-operation and participation, but it is essentially the work of God. God always makes the first move; if He chooses not to act then all of man's organisation is fruitless in producing vital, growing spiritual life.

Biblical teaching and the small group

The Scriptures give some guidelines for Christian small groups which, if followed, would avoid many of the pitfalls which have caused some groups to fail.

John Kleinig in his book discusses the rationale of Christian small group activity and points out that we must not neglect "several significant aspects of Biblical teaching". These are (abridged and adapted):

"1. **The formation of small groups in a Christian context is primarily a response to the call of God.** Group life is seen in scripture as part of God's pattern for his people, and not merely some sociological necessity.

"2. **Techniques are subordinate to the message** . . . the impact of Christian teaching is to be found in its content rather than its mode of presentation. Where too much attention is given to techniques there is a superficial enthusiasm, a high 'mortality rate' and the kind of faith which wilts in isolation. For such, group activity is not a means of growth in faith; it exhausts the content of faith.

"3. **Communication of the message is fundamentally a work of the Holy Spirit** . . . What this means is that whatever aids we might employ in our endeavours to communicate or to discuss profitably the Christian message, they will be of no avail unless the Holy Spirit is at work in the hearts and minds of the people involved."

16

"4. **Success or fruitfulness is a gift of God.**" Dr. Kleinig stresses another theological perspective which he considers deserves attention. He says: "Doctrine and practice are intimately intertwined. Thus Paul, when speaking of Christian behaviour, speaks of the fruit of the Spirit — of what grows naturally out of a life response to the Spirit's work."[5]

Groups do not cause spiritual renewal. The structure and the dynamics of a group seeking God's leadership provide an atmosphere conducive to growth, discovery of gifts, commitment and service. Renewal must not be seen as a result of participation in a group, but as a by-product — a gift which God often bestows upon those who seek Him.

The basic purpose of a Christian group

While we have learnt much from the behavioural sciences, the specialists in group dynamics and the human potential movement, about group process and techniques, we need always to be aware that small groups which meet in the name of Christ will have some goals which are quite different and distinctive. Frequently there will be similar purposes to those groups without a specific Christian orientation but the means and the motivation of achieving them will often vary. It is well to keep before a Christian group its basic purposes. In evaluating its shared life these can be a helpful objective criteria against which it can measure its life.

The prime purpose of all Christian community is to **honour our Lord and God.** "Where two or three are gathered together in my name — there am I in the midst." Christ is central to each group not to create a "nice" atmosphere or to increase the therapeutic qualities of the group, nor even to be a vague unifying factor in the fellowship. He is not there to be used but to be worshipped.

Our primary function is not to serve each other but to worship God. The church is not a collection of folk associated because they share a common interest in religion, but the fellowship of those whom God called into His "*koinonia*" (fellowship) with Himself through Christ and in Him with one another. "*Koinonia*" has a horizontal reference simply and solely because it has a vertical one. It is not possible to maintain the vertical reference while rejecting the horizontal.

The Lord's Prayer is a prayer for a group. Each request is in the plural 'our'. Well we might pray when we come to "hallowed be thy Name" — "may your name be honoured, made holy, in the midst of our small group and through us, collectively and individually, to our community".

The next purpose of the group is **to minister to each other.** Christ's new commandment was "to love just as I have loved you". As He participates fully in our lives so we are to become deeply involved in the lives of others. Motivated by Christ's love we are to be deeply concerned for the needs of each member of our small group. The Holy Spirit will then work through our gifts to nurture and mature. The small group is a vital aid to spiritual growth through mutual ministry within the group.

> "Such involvement need not take place in the small group. But the small group has sprung to prominence today because so many of us have not been involved in others' lives! The impersonalization and depersonalisation of our society has struck deeply into the life of the Church and robbed us of our heart and warmth. To love Jesus' way, we have to really know and really care about one another as persons. It is precisely the awareness of lost contact with others that has led so many to join or form groups."[6]

A distinctive new emphasis in small groups today is not upon each person using the group to meet his or her own personal needs but to make oneself accessible and available to God and to the members of one's group. That is having our gifts set free by God for the need of the other person and the world.

Another important function of the Christian group is to **unite Christians in their common cause.** In the process of being involved deeply in each others' lives the group members become aware that they are more than an association of individuals. They become aware of a group identity.

We have all been cast in the mould of our respective cultural background — the set of which it is hard to break out. The emphasis in western civilisation upon individualism is contrary to Christian teaching. The collectiveness of Communism comes closer to the Christian ideal but with the important fundamental difference that true Christian community results from love.

The final dimension of group function is **the preparation of its members for mission in the world.** A group can become ingrown. It can become exclusive rather than inclusive. One of the common criticisms of small groups is that they can so easily become "holy huddles", "self-righteous cliques" or 'self improvement societies". The group experience can be so significant that the needs of others are neglected. A group which is alive in the Spirit will seek together to live God's Word resulting in a sharing of faith and an overflow of love to others.

"To neglect the social is to be more "spiritual" than Jesus Christ had been . . . The core of the Gospel was not that the Word became Spirit, but that the Word became flesh and this meant that the Gospel had to be expressed in very human terms, in terms of social action, in terms of flesh and blood. Words alone were not enough."[7]

These then are the elements of a Christian group which need to be held in balance. It is a delicate balance which is difficult to maintain. Where each function is fulfilled, excesses will be avoided and such a group will accomplish the basic tasks of the Body of Christ.

Characteristics of Christian small groups today

There are a number of distinctive characteristics of the small group movement in the church today.

The first is that there is an **acceptance that they are fundamental to vital Christian life.** Nearly ten years ago when I observed the small group movement in many countries and situations, to many it was quite new and the element of experimentation was predominant. Whereas the question then was "Shall we launch into small groups?" in recent observations overseas the question I heard most was "Which type of small group will best suit the needs of our particular situation?" They are now no longer looked upon by the majority as an optional activity. The focus is now upon the nature and purpose of small groups, how to use them most effectively.

The nature of leadership has been re-defined. There has been a shift in the centre of authority. Once there was a designated leader — now the emphasis is upon all having leadership roles. The concern today is with helping all members of the Body of Christ (clergy and laity) grasp the concept of mutuality of ministry and how to enable this to happen. *"Charisma"* in leadership is available to all God's people. The role of the up front charismatic leader is still a valid one; however the emphasis is more upon the leader being a facilitator or enabler. The group may have an elected or designated leader, but direction grows out of the group.

There is a **greater emphasis upon relationships.** The "human potential movement" is seen by many as part of God's judgement on the church because the church forgot that it was to be an open, supportive, concerned fellowship. As was Christian Science a judgement when we forgot to be a healing group and the secular social action movement when we forgot we are called to love all the world. The human potential movement's emphasis upon feelings, honesty, vulnerability and confrontation are being used to help many groups enter new depths in their relationships.

New, appropriate, learning methods are being used. While inductive methods have been used in many groups from the early days of the modern small group movement in the church, there is a new concern about the feeding in of content. The appropriate time in the learning experience for this content to be studied is important — finding the "teachable moment", when the group will best benefit from it.

Many groups in their new sense of freedom and sharing floundered in subjectivism and a sharing of ignorance. The role of the resource person and the place of Bible study is being re-discovered. The relevance of studies for the everyday living of the participants is being emphasized. Relational Bible studies such as those developed by Lyman Coleman in his *Serendipity* books and *Find Your Self in the Bible* by Karl A. Olsson are helping in this search for relevance.

The need to belong to more than one "Ekklesia" or gathering of Christians. While there is in many senses a renewed emphasis upon the local congregation, there is also a trend developing away from a narrow or inward-looking 'congregationalism' which restricts one's spiritual growth to the local congregation. A significant number of Christians are looking for opportunities to broaden their spiritual experiences through gathering together with others in Christ's name on a regular basis in small groups. This helps transcend denominational barriers and gives a wider perspective of the Body of Christ. One person, or couple may be a loyal member of the local church and leaders of a house cell but they may also be members of another small group in their neighbourhood or place of work.

Small groups are playing an **important role in outreach.** The small house-centred neighbourhood group is bringing a warmth and intimacy to evangelism which was absent in most large gatherings in the past. In the Dialogue Evangelism groups, Lay Witness Missions, supper groups and other informal neighbourhood groups people are finding Christ. Outreach youth ministries which are succeeding have at their heart a deeply committed close-knit, covenanted small group of young people.

There is a new concern for meditation and contemplation. In the second book in this series *Creative Ideas for Small Groups* I have developed this more fully. Many of the Catholic masters in this field, such as Thomas Merton, are being studied and their methods practised. The use of silence in the group and in retreat situations is an art for most protestants to re-discover.

The division of small groups into age groups is being discarded. Intergenerational groupings are being used with adults and young people meeting together. The idealism and enthusiasm of the young people and the maturity of the adults is bringing a new dimension to many groups.

Families are finding new levels of relationships as they meet in specially structured experiences and discover their small group role. Family Effectiveness Training and resources for family groups prepared by Lyman Coleman are helping many family units find a new level of fellowship as they learn to exercise their mutuality of ministry in the home. Family clustering as developed by people like Margaret Sawin in the U.S.A. is bringing new life to families as they live out their life in the wider context of a number of families.

The role of small groups as a **structure of hope** is a significant characteristic of the modern small group in the church of today and the near uncertain future. At a conference led by Gordon Cosby of the Church of the Saviour, Washington D.C. which I attended recently, he began by figuratively wearing the mantle of a prophet of doom. Drawing from Heilbroner's *Inquiry into the Human Prospect* he drew our attention to the underlying anxiety of humankind as we face the inevitable environmental collapse if unrestricted growth continues. The question thoughtful people are asking

"Is there hope for man?" is met by the cynicism of pessimists, with a defeated "No!" But what of the Christian? Cosby exhorted, "we must face it and seek solutions in new global structures. As we live through the anxiety bordering on panic we must be aware of the temptations of sitting it out or to conform as much as possible or to withdraw from deep involvement with those who suffer. As Christians we can exude hope as we remain close to our Lord. We must build structures of hope." The small group will play a vital role in giving support, encouraging one another and drawing close to Christ. Together the group must be involved in helping alleviate the suffering of the oppressed. Large monolithic structures will collapse, but small Christ centred structures will survive and be citadels of hope.

References

1. Lawrence O. Richards, *A New Face for the Church* (Zondervan, Michigan, 1970), p.153.
2. John Kleinig, *The Group — Its Nature and Role* (Anzea, Sydney, 1974), p.7.
3. C. W. Shead, *How to Develop a Praying Church* (Abingdon Press, 1964), p. 12-13.
4. Samuel M. Shoemaker, *With the Holy Spirit and With Fire* (Harper & Row, New York and Evanston, 1960), p.110.
5. *The Group — Its Nature and Role*, pp.3-5.
6. Lawrence O. Richards, *69 Ways to Start a Study Group and Keep it Growing* (Zondervan, 1973), pp. 11, 12.
7. Bruce Kendrick, *Come out of the Wilderness* (Collins, 1973).

Other books consulted—
John L. Casteel, *Spiritual Renewal through Small Groups* (Association Press, NY, 1957).
Michael Skinner, *House Groups* (Epworth Press & SPCK, 1969).

2 The Small Group in the New Testament Church

Athol Gill

In his stylized presentation of the progress of the Gospel from Jerusalem to Rome (Acts 1.8), Luke describes two focal points in the Church's mission: the temple (centre and symbol of the old which was even then passing away) and the home (centre and symbol of the new which was shortly to replace it).

"With one mind they kept up their daily attendance at the temple and, breaking bread in private houses, shared their meals with unaffected joy, as they praised God and enjoyed the favour of the whole people." (2.46-47).

"And every day they went steadily on with their teaching in the temple and in private houses, telling the good news of Jesus the Messiah." (Acts 5.42).

These two passages are summaries drawn up by Luke as "a representation of the way of life of the Christian community" (Haenchen).[1] They depict the early Christian community as gathering at two fixed points, the temple and the home. They describe private houses as centres of worship and hospitality, of Christian teaching and missionary proclamation.

In order to appreciate the importance of these two focal points in Luke's presentation of the early life of the community we must first understand the role which he ascribes to the temple.

Luke depicts salvation history as divided into three **The temple** periods: the time of Israel (Luke 1-2), the time of Jesus **and the** (Luke 3-24) and the time of the Church (Acts). The temple **Christian** is the motif of theological continuity which holds the three **community** periods together.

In the birth stories (Luke 1-2) all of the characters portrayed are models of Jewish piety. Their religious life revolves around the temple in Jerusalem which is described as the place of sacred service (Luke 1.8-9), sacrifice (Luke 1.10, 2.22, 24), prayer (Luke 1.10; 2.37), fasting (Luke 2.37), and teaching (Luke 2.46), the headquarters of the devout group who were looking for the redemption of Israel (Luke 2.25, 38). In his description of the ministry of Jesus, Luke emphasizes that Jesus made the temple, the centre of Israelite worship, the centre of an extended teaching ministry to the people of Israel (Luke 19, 47-21.38). The Gospel ends, as it begins, with the worshipping community in the temple. After the ascension the disciples return to Jerusalem with great joy and spend their time in the temple blessing God (Luke 24, 52-53).

So then, in the Gospel the temple has become, for Luke, the centre of continuity between Israel (Luke 1-2), the ministry of Jesus (Luke 19.47-21.38) and the Christian community (Luke 24, 52-53), with the Christian community (Luke 24.52-53) taking over the role previously ascribed to the community of Israel (Luke 1-2).

These themes continue over into the Book of Acts where it is said that the apostles, and indeed the whole Christian community, daily went up to the temple to pray (Acts 2.46; 3.1-10), and where it is emphasized that the temple was the centre of their ministry of preaching (Acts 2.14ff.; 3.11ff.) and teaching (Acts 4.2; 5.20-21).

But, a change is coming for, as we have already seen, in two of the important summary representations of the life of the early Church (Acts 2.46-47; 5.42) the private home is placed alongside the temple. Private homes are depicted as becoming increasingly centres of worship and hospitality, of Christian teaching and missionary proclamation.

As the story of the early Church continues to unfold, Luke describes homes being used for "prayer meetings (Acts 12.12), for an evening of Christian fellowship (Acts 21.7), for Holy Communion services (Acts 2.46), for a whole night of prayer, worship and instruction (Acts 20.7), for impromptu evangelistic gatherings (Acts 16.32), for planned meetings in order to hear the Christian gospel (Acts 10.22), for following up enquiries (Acts 18.26), for organized instruction (Acts 5.42)."[2]

What is happening in Acts is that as the Church's missionary activity takes it outwards away from Jerusalem, spurred on in this direction by persecution at the centre, the focal point of its activity becomes, increasingly, private houses.

To be sure, Paul returns to the temple when he delivers the collection for the poor Christians in Jerusalem. He even undergoes the Nazarite vow of purification as suggested by James and the Jerusalem elders (Acts 21.26ff.). But, the fate of Israel and the temple is sealed. Paul's "orthodoxy" is not accepted by the Jews, there is a riot and he is rescued by the soldiers and eventually sent to Rome for trial (Acts 21.27ff.). In a rented house in Rome, after further unsuccessful attempts to convince the Jews about Jesus and the kingdom of God, Paul pronounces judgment upon Israel, declaring that God is going to the Gentiles — "they will listen" (Acts 28.23ff.).

This is the end for Israel. By the time Luke has undertaken to write his two volumes, Jerusalem and the temple have been destroyed and the Christian church has spread throughout the Gentile world, meeting everywhere in the house of its members.

**The home
as a basis
for outreach**

"Peter's mission at Caesarea, regarded by Luke as one of the great turning-points in his story in Acts, and so described at length forms a bridge from one mission to the other (from the Jewish world to the Graeco-Roman world)".[3] Cornelius, "a religious man, he and his whole family joined in the worship of God", had a vision while praying in his house and was told that he should send for Peter who was lodging with another Simon, a tanner "whose house is by the sea".

Peter, praying on the roof of the house, also received a vision and when messengers arrived from Cornelius he accompanied them to Caesarea. Cornelius had called together his relatives and close friends, a sermon is preached, the Holy Spirit comes upon those who listened and they are baptized in the name of Jesus Christ (Acts 10).

The house and the household have become the basis for evangelistic activity in the early church.

A similar situation is revealed in the story of the Philippian gaoler, where Paul and Silas spoke "the word of the Lord to him and to all that were in his house", so that "all the household believed in God" and were baptized (Acts 16.25ff.).

A different situation is seen, however, in the description of events following the beheading of James and the arrest of Peter. We are told that Peter was rescued from Herod's clutches and that "he made for the house of Mary, the mother of John Mark, where a large company were at prayer" (Acts 12.12).

The house and the household have also become the centre of liturgical activity in the early church.

A further development may be seen when Paul's evangelistic activity takes him to Europe. In Philippi, where he preaches on European soil for the first time, he stays in the home of Lydia who has been baptized, with her household, after "the Lord had opened her heart" (Acts 16.11ff.). During his time in Corinth, Paul lodged with Priscilla and Aquila and worked with them in their trade of tentmaking (Acts 18.1ff.). Later, he sends greetings to the "church in their house" (Rom. 16.5).

The house and the household have been the centre of hospitality and fellowship in the early church.

This use of private houses was undoubtedly a development of **the missionary strategy of Jesus.** At the beginning of his public ministry Mark tells us that after Jesus left the synagogue he "entered the house of Simon and Andrew with James and John" (Mark 1.28). After Jesus healed Peter's mother-in-law, the home seems to have become a base of operations for the whole city gathered at the door so that he could heal the sick (Acts 2.1). This home appears to have been the location of several incidents in his ministry.

When Jesus sent out the Twelve on mission He commanded them, "When you enter a house, stay there until you leave the place". The household, then, was the potential nucleus of believers. But there is always the obverse side to the offer of salvation. If the household refused to hear, the disciples are commanded "shake off the dust of your feet as a testimony against them" for they have failed to respond to the grace of God and have thus denied their calling and failed to realize their potential in the kingdom of God (Mark 6.7-13).

The missionary strategy of Jesus

According to Luke, when Jesus sent out the Seventy on mission, He gave them the command, "Whatever house you enter, first say, 'Peace be to this house!' And if a son of peace is there, your peace will rest upon him." But again there is the potential threat: "Whenever you enter a town and they do not receive you, go into the streets and say, 'Even the dust of your town which clings to our feet, we wipe off against you; nevertheless know that the kingdom of God has come near to you." (Luke 10.1ff.). As the grace of God and His peace finds a lodging place in the hearts of men, so the new community is established as the household turns to God, through Jesus, in repentance and faith.

To some extent, of course, it may be argued that when Jesus used houses for preaching and teaching, for healing and for fellowship, He was only displaying what might be termed "a normal sensitivity to the contemporary social structures of life". But, it seems certain that there is a deeper meaning as well. For Jesus, the old Jewish distinctions had been abolished for the good news of the kingdom belonged to all. The grace and peace of God belonged not only to pious male Israelites, but included the lepers who had to live outside the camp regarded as "unclean" and denied fellowship with others, the Gentiles who had no share in the privileges of Israel, the women and the children who had no status within the community. With Jesus the potential of salvation was extended to all members of the household and this contemporary social structure took on a new meaning under the impact of the Gospel.

Household churches

It is, therefore, not surprising that when we pass over to *the Book of Acts,* and *the Letters of Paul* we should find a number of references to the Gospel coming to a whole household. When Peter went up to Jerusalem and recounted what had happened at Caesarea he included mention of Cornelius' vision in which the angel told him to send for the apostle who would "declare to you a message by which you will be saved, you and all your household." (Acts 11.14). At Philippi, Lydia was baptized "with her household" after "the Lord opened her heart to hear what was said by Paul" (Acts 16.14-15). Similarly, Paul told the Philippian gaoler, "Believe in the Lord Jesus, and you will be saved, you and your household" and the account concludes with the note that the gaoler "rejoiced with all his household that he had believed in God" (Acts 16.31,34). During Paul's lengthy Corinthian ministry Crispus, the ruler of the synagogue, "believed in the Lord, together with all his household" (Acts 18.8). Paul himself mentions that he had baptized "the household of Stephanus" (1 Cor. 1.16).

It is in line with this concept of the Christian household that we find a number of references to "household churches". In Romans 16.5 Paul sends greetings to Prisca and Aquila and "the church which is in their house" and when he writes to the Corinthians he mentions that "Aquila and Prisca, together with the church in their house, send hearty greetings in the Lord". (1 Cor. 16.19). In concluding his letter to the Colossians, Paul asks the church there to give his greetings to the church at Laodicea and to Nympha "and the church in her house" (Col. 4.15). Paul's letter to Philemon, though primarily private correspondence, is addressed nonetheless to "Philemon, our beloved fellow worker and Apphia our sister and Archippus our fellow soldier, and the church in your house" (Phlm 2). A similar situation is probably to be inferred in Romans 16.15: "Greet Philologus, Julia, Nereus and his sister, and Olympas, and all the saints who are with them."

It is almost certain that every mention of a local church or of a church meeting, whether for worship or fellowship, is in actual fact a reference to a house church situation.

Again, this is not to be thought of as merely a sociological necessity forced upon the early Christians by economic considerations. It is also theological. "Primitive Christianity structured its congregations in families, groups and 'houses'. The house was both a fellowship and a place of meeting . . . The house and family are the smallest natural groups in the total structure of the congregation."[4] In the New Testament man is understood as a communal being and the primary communal relationship for the Christian, as for others, was the household. Since the good news abolished all artificial distinctions based on race, sex and class the Christian household became the communal unit par excellence. Master and slave, husband and wife, Jew and Gentile, parents and children became a unity in Christ (cf. Gal. 3.28; Eph. 2). This new-found unity of the communal unit formed the nucleus of the earliest Christian communities.

Against this background the "household codes" (Col. 3.18ff.; Eph. 5.22ff.; 1 Pet. 2.18ff.) takes on even deeper significance, as do the directions in the Pastorals that deacons should take good care of their children and houses (1 Tim. 3.12) and that bishops must rule their own houses well for if they cannot do that it is unlikely that they will be able to care for the whole congregation (1 Tim. 3:4-5).

It is also against this background that we should interpret the passages with which we began.

Acts 2.46-47: "With one mind they kept up their daily attendance at the temple and, breaking bread in private houses, shared their meals with unaffected joy, as they praised God and enjoyed the favour of the whole people."

Acts 5.42: "And everyday they went steadily on with their teaching in the temple and in private houses, telling the good news of Jesus the Messiah."

Acts 20.20: "I did not shrink from declaring to you anything that was profitable, and teaching you in public and from house to house, testifying both to Jew and to Greeks of repentance to God and faith in our Lord Jesus Christ."

Public proclamation and household worship and instruction were integral parts of the dynamic of the early Christian mission, with the new unity of the extended family forming the nucleus of the community.

References:

1. Ernst Haenchen, *The Acts of the Apostles* (Blackwell, Oxford, 1971).
2. Michael Green, *Evangelism in the Early Church* (Hodder & Stoughton, London, 1971), p. 218.
3. B. S. Brown, "Missionary Structures in the Early Church" *(Tyndale Papers* No. 3, 1965).
4. O. Michel, *Theological Dictionary of the New Testament* (translated G. Bromiley, Eerdmans, Grand Rapids).

"Change and decay in all around I see," says the pessimist. "I see in change," says the optimist, "the opportunity to create something worthwhile."

3   Change in the Local Church through Small Groups

Ross Kingham

We all tend to fear change on a large or small scale in our lives. There is not one generation of men which has not divided into those who resisted change with all their might and those who have welcomed it.

We are living in a time of development and change. This movement is reflected not only in our society, but in the church. "Congregation after congregation is struggling with problems caused by new ways in today's world, new patterns of life which do not fit a church whose services and functions are carried over from a horse and buggy culture."[1]

Unfortunately we tend to think that if we change the ways in which we have always done things our standards will decline. But in a large measure change is intrinsic to the Christian faith. Many of us have had to change our way of thinking, our way of life, to follow Christ.

If we agree that change in the church is not to be feared but welcomed, we have to examine ways in which change can be encouraged and utilized. We must then establish what we feel is the basic aim of the church — and in this context I am talking about the local fellowship of believers.

I believe our basic aim is to share Christ's life to- **The basic aim** gether, of nurturing believers. There may be many who **of the church** would disagree — what about evangelism? What about social action? What about the maintenance of community traditions? Certainly these are important but I am convinced that nothing must obscure our primary aim. Once this is established we have a base on which to build. "Let us hold fast the confession of our hope without wavering, for he who promised is faithful; and let us consider how to stir up one another to love and good works, not neglecting to meet together, but encouraging one another, and all the more as you see the Day drawing near." (Hebrews 10:23-25).

We cannot recreate New Testament churches. Rather than striving to return to New Testament **forms** or patterns we should aim at returning to the New Testament **insights and emphases.** Paul in Ephesians 4:11ff. writes:

> *"And his gifts were that some should be apostles, some prophets, some evangelists, some pastors and teachers, for the equipment of the saints, for the work of ministry, for building up the body of Christ, until we all attain to the unity of the faith and of the knowledge of the Son of God, to mature manhood, to the measure of the stature of the fullness of Christ . . . "*

We can use these insights into the nature and function of a church to reshape our own patterns of church life, "so as to be fully responsive to the patterns of life of the members of the congregation".[2] **The church is basically people in relationship** — not primarily meetings, agencies and programmes. Change therefore cannot be imposed from outside but has to be dealt with by an individual congregation. As they share in the life of Christ, possessing the Holy Spirit, the whole congregation can grow and change. In this growth process relationships are developed and consolidated, as Christians minister to each other in the Spirit. The meetings or assemblies of the congregation must be flexible and adaptable to enable these things to happen.

Evangelism and service will follow this type of development and change in a church. Individual members of groups in the church will be involved in evangelism as an expression of their love for Christ. Others will be involved in service. Ideally all the secondary functions of the church will be intertwined. We have to proclaim Christ and basis to this proclamation is an acting out of our beliefs.

Change, tension and resistance

It is a tragic mistake to think you can automatically generate changes in peoples' norms, values and life-attitudes simply by altering forms or structures. Tensions will occur as change takes place in a church. There is little we can do to avoid the conflict which is inherent between traditional and new life-styles, even where both life-styles are Christian. We can cushion the blow and we must strive to make sure what we are trying to share is clearly explained. We are all to human, even if we are all Spirit-filled Christians, and we are conditioned by the past.

In his book, *A Leader and the Process of Change,* Thomas A. Barnett talks of the positive value of resistance to change. Resistance to change forces a clarification of the **purpose** of change and the results to be achieved. It discloses inadequate communication processes and deficiencies in the flow of information. It helps modify plans for change to give a greater benefit. (Resistance brings into the open possibly unexpected consequences of a decision). Barnett emphasises that resistance to change can be handled without destroying the unity of a group. Richards[3] points out that in the church there can be no question of "divorce on the grounds of incompatibility".

Change and the small group

I am convinced that the small group design fulfils many of the requirements of a church's need for nurture of its members. It is based on mutual ministry, on building its members up in faith. As soon as we begin to involve ourselves in establishing small groups within a church change begins to occur.

I have emphasized that change in the church reflects in many changes change in our world, in our society. There is a need among people today to share in community, to get close to other people. Having achieved this many find something missing and move further to find the deeper fellowship — a knowledge of and close relationship with God. For this person the small group situation is ideal.

However, enthusiastic as we may be to introduce small groups into the church, and therefore automatically inducing change, we need to examine and re-examine our motives.

People committed to the small group concept must empathize with the person totally involved in the traditional church pattern. It is very easy to condemn people as being rigid, old-fashioned. We may find that we come into conflict with the 'traditionalists' in our church. This conflict may

33

be suppressed, or degenerate to a guerilla-type war (complete with snipers) or it may include face-to-face disagreement, with lobbying before parish or congregational meetings so that people can take sides.

We must be aware of the danger of substituting means for ends. We may enjoy our involvement in the organizational machinery (even small groups) to the extent that our zeal and devotion to Christ is deflected to fostering 'our/my show'. We have to examine our **methods**, our approaches to people. We may speak our convictions freely but we must not try to manipulate people, and we must make sure we do not speak with an aura of superiority. We have to demonstrate our respect and trust to those who disagree, and our warmth of fellow-feeling as Christians.

The Christian who clings to the past, to traditions is still one of us. We are **one Body.** "How dare we separate ourselves from him, tearing the Body apart in our eagerness for change," writes Richards. Paul said to people involved in a similar conflict: while you divide yourselves from your brothers and deny the unity God asserts "are you not unspiritual?" (Much of the first chapters of 1 Corinthians would appear to be addressed to very keen small group supporters!)

Leadership in our churches must provide opportunities for creative change to take place. There is a tendency in both lay and clerical leaders to resist change for what seem to them perfectly good and valid reasons. Alternatively church leaders cannot **force** change, for it never lasts.

If there are a number of small group enthusiasts in a church you will find it a worthwhile exercise to perform a role play and become people who object to the introduction of small groups. You may find that your imaginary people just do not want to know about them. You may find they recall past failures to introduce new concepts or techniques. You may find that the participants reveal they feel threatened by change, or that they fear it means the same old workhorses will have to do the work, or be leaders, or organizers. **Objections to change**

You may find a reluctance in the person playing the minister to delegate authority or responsibility for church members' nurture or guidance. You may find people saying there is no room in the church programme for something new. You may find people saying they do not want little holy huddles dotted around the church, wallowing in subjectivity.

Having verbalized many of the objections how do you deal with them? Successful change in a church depends on the personal spiritual growth of the members and their sense of freedom to take part openly and honestly in the on-going process. At heart I believe we all want to be free, to grow. But to be actually given the challenge, the opportunity can be a shattering experience.

Most of our fellow congregation members may appear fixed in their societal, their community, their home and their church roles. I would particularly plead for understanding for one of the people most fixed in a role — the clergyman. For many clergy the small group idea is a totally new one. These men need our love and understanding. They need to know that we are not criticizing their ministry if we are enthusiastic about small groups.

Another factor which militates against inducing change through small groups is that our church buildings are not designed for coping with the pattern. Some pew backs are so high you cannot turn round to see the person behind you. If you try to alter the physical design of the church you are once again cutting across tradition or the fact that the basic floor plan of a church cannot be changed without ripping the whole thing apart.

There is a temptation for the small group proponents to move out of the local church fellowship. This solves or avoids conflict, but it means that the small group cannot merge with the larger body of believers. Alternatively, even where there are a number of different types of small groups in a church, there will be some church members who will totally stand outside them, or even withdraw (hopefully temporarily) from the church.

The results of change

What are the obvious results of change? It should be demonstrated in the personal, spiritual growth of members and their sense of freedom to take part openly and honestly in the change process. We must realise that the results of change in a congregation may largely be unknown. We must not be preoccupied with specific formed structures.

We could go back to our parishes from a small groups course and set the goal of **x** number of study groups, **y** number of witness cells, **z** number of youth cells and so on. But we must resist that temptation to try to **direct**

35

change or to force it into pre-determined channels. Rather, we are to be flexible and open as individual Christians, and work to create opportunities for change (of whatever form or structure) to take place.

Encourage, and pray for, the minister and leaders in your church, that they may be able to provide opportunities for creative change to take place. Church leaders tend either to freeze out such opportunities; or to go to the other extreme and move unwisely, forcing change and manipulating its course in the congregation. Forced change is never lasting!

Ideally, where a **congregation** is spiritually open and alive, it ought to be involved in decisions that affect its life, including the provision of opportunities for small groups comprising some of its members, to operate. Again, ideally, this decision by the congregation ought to be one of consensus (not majority vote, and not by an autocratically imposed stipulation). That is, that particular congregation, as a Body of Christ, agrees unanimously to establish small groups and work and pray for their success. This would involve the active, prayerful goodwill of even those who remain out of small groups.

In practice, generally a congregation needs the guidance of the leaders/elders/deacons. These people, with the support of the minister, need to be able to stimulate 'prior-experience' programmes so small groups can be experienced and evaluated. (e.g. there could be a six-week series of studies; a Retreat using small groups; a parish delegation to a small group course). Congregations need such 'prior-experience' programmes so they can get the feel of small group life, so they can then respond to suggestions for change on the basis of real understanding. Such a threat-reducing procedure takes much of the fear out of the projected change.

The success of change depends on the individual growth of church members, and on their ability to share fully and freely in the change process. Change, then, must be geared towards providing opportunities for mutual ministry, for the development and exercise of the gifts of all God's people involved in the change process. Such change is Spirit-directed and Christ-honouring.

References:
1. Lawrence A. Richards, *A New Face for the Church* (Zondervan, Grand Rapids, 1970), pp. 66, 69.
2. *A New Face for the Church*, p. 144.
3. *A New Face for the Church*, p. 210.

4   Types of Small Groups

There are many kinds of small groups that function within the church. In the main, if they are in any way vital they have one common factor — they exist to meet the needs of the persons involved. Because individual needs differ greatly so do the range of groups which have emerged to meet these needs. In a real sense they cannot be ranked in order of importance. "A group finds validity in its ability to meet the needs of the persons involved."

In our basic small group training course I have given time during the first session for the participants to reflect upon the small group experiences in which they have been involved prior to attending the course. This is done to build confidence as they recognize they have had previous experience of small group life and, therefore, will be resource persons in the inductive learning throughout the course. It further helps them to appreciate the wide variety of groups in which people naturally group in everyday living. A collation of some of this feed-in helps establish this last point.

Minister's sharing group
Discussion
Visiting
Healing Prayer Group
Committee
All Age Church School
Married Couples
Sharing — Prayer
Confirmation Classes
Bible Study Discussion
Family Fellowships
Service Projects
Surfies Groups
Orientation Group
Youth Cells
Arts Group
Nurture Groups
Outreach
Migrants
Crafts — Art
Koinonia

Youth Fellowship
Young Marrieds
Women's Fellowship or
  Guild
Sports
Ministers' Wives
Workshop Days
School Discussions
Natural Teen Grouping—
  peers
Musical Groups
Coffee House Teams
Ecumenical House Group
Inter-School Christian
  Fellowship
Knitting
'At Home' — Welcoming
  Group
Family
Recreational
Camp Study Group

Dialogue	Group Therapy
Camps — Counsellors	Theatre Group
Parish Fellowship Day	Tutorials
Open Hour	Discovery Group
Dinner Parties	Working Bees
Marriage Enrichment	Office Group
Coffee times	Union Meeting
Couples	Family

Some of the more common categories of small groups found in the Christian Church are given here. In practice they have their own unique characteristics.

Friendship or contact groups

These vary in size and regularity of meetings. Often they meet weekly (or bi-weekly) giving the invited persons an opportunity to meet others, generally their peers, in an unstructured setting where little is required of them. There is general conversation, the sharing of an interest, or participation in a general activity where the individual can choose to participate or not. They are designed to establish relationships, with the group setting the pace and type of discussion, e.g. businessman's luncheon meeting, housewives' morning tea, etc. Spiritual depth may come later, particularly if the leader is sensitive to the needs of the group.

Interest groups

People meet in these groups who have a common need or interest. They may meet together to develop certain skills, e.g. manual, relationships, educational or social skills. Some groups for parents meet to gain insights in understanding teenagers or young adults may meet in preparation for marriage. Some may just be concerned with developing a manual skill. There is generally a specific effort made to build a sense of inclusiveness that will lead to a feeling of acceptance and understanding of each other.

Social groups

These groups vary in size and regularity of meeting. They may be open or closed groups, depending on the purpose and constituency. These groups are generally self-selective, give a sense of "belonging", meet for fun and pleasure and are self-supportive in a social way, with a constant turnover of members in the group occurring without fuss.

Discussion/ study groups

These may be short or long term programmes. Whether they are single, brief weekend encounters or weekly meetings, they help encourage personal growth and human interaction in exciting ways. These groups specifically include a sense of commitment to group life, focus on something of value beyond 'just meeting', concern for each other and a more deliberate sharing of personal values. Books that consider biblical, historical, theological, sociological, psychological and other current affairs are often used as a starting point for discussion. Often these groups share a common discipline.

Therapy groups

The word simply means 'healing'. It implies soundness, wholeness and freedom. It permits people to explore their "hang-ups" in a controlled environment and gives them the choice to change their behavioural patterns if they so choose. These groups often last two years and are closed groups (i.e. by invitation only). Trained professional leadership is necessary for most types and a strong commitment by members for regular attendance is very important. Feelings are freely exposed while a supportive group offers sensitive feedback. Some therapy groups are general or social, e.g. weight watchers, while others are closer to in-depth therapy groups, e.g. Alcoholics Anonymous and certain Recovery Groups such as "Grow".

Bible study groups

I would question the value of studying the Bible as is without relating it to real life situations. The Bible wasn't given to us to study just academically — it is the record of God revealing Himself and His intention to mankind. It is meant to produce change in people's minds and character. Change will not necessarily be produced by just studying the content, we have to struggle with the relevance of the truth for life situations. Some Bible study can become purely academic and intellectual in its approach without being relevant or relational. We must beware of becoming introverted and limited in our approach.

These are established forms of church small groups. **Prayer groups**
Unfortunately prayer groups have not always had the best
image in the church because they have become ingrown
or stereotyped but that does not mean that all prayer groups
have been ineffective. We need to show the world today
a new interest in prayer. Some creative prayer fellowships
have developed where the old forms are being replaced by
some exciting innovations.

These are similar to encounter and therapy groups. **Sharing/**
They are supportive groups where people share pressures, **fellowship**
doubts, fears, successes, failures, etc. Essentially, they are **group**
designed to find people who care enough to listen to each
other and who have enough genuine concern to provide
support for one another, particularly as they venture into
new areas of openness in sharing of themselves. Sharing
groups need to be tied in closely with some kind of study
content, especially of the Word of God, otherwise it will
become a purely subjective thing and suffer greatly because
of that. That objectivity needs to be brought in to give it
the kind of balance it would need.

This is one of the newest and largest developments in **Personal**
the Christian Church. Some Yokefellow groups are a good **growth**
illustration of a personal growth group. They seek to find **group**
out where they are really at, as far as their personal growth
is concerned; one method is by the use of self evaluation
sheets. Each member receives and completes an evaluation
form which is then returned to Headquarters where a clinical
psychologist evaluates it and then sends comments back.
The individual may then share as much as he wishes with
the group. The groups only commence because a group of
people are prepared to submit themselves to this kind of
discipline. It is not superimposed upon the group — everyone has to be prepared to become involved in this and
to enter into the openness, sharing and concern required
of those in this situation. They use *Prayer Can Change Your
Life* by J. J. Packer as one of their text books.

Personal growth groups take many different forms but
there is essentially a clear contract entered into with each
other and deep levels of trust and openness required.

Koinonia group

The name describes the quality of the life the Christian Church is supposed to experience. The koinonia group is used for most of these aspects we have already mentioned. Prayer, study, sharing, personal growth, outreach — are all aspects of the koinonia group. This group is an ideal one for the Christian Church because if it is a true koinonia group it covers all facets of Christian life with a balance between all.

Task group

These groups have a specific function to fulfil which does not necessarily involve the personal needs of its members. Usually set up to undertake some task, e.g. a committee set up to plan, oversee or initiate an activity.

Outreach group

It is similar to a task group. The outreach may cover two main areas say, outreach and evangelism or outreach and social concern. In both the 'Contact' group plays an important part. This aspect is discussed later in this book. In the evangelistic outreach group are low key approaches to people through the contact group and then various stages following that are described. Then there is the more direct forms of evangelistic use of groups; for example, a lay witness weekend or the dialogue evangelism groups. The social action group may be just a contact group of people showing concern for a social need in their community. It may be a more long term group seeing how they can bring about change in their community and formulating a programme for change to change the very structures of the local community.

Some General Distinctions

In understanding the different types of groups it helps to make some **general distinction between groups.**

Spontaneous or organised groups

These commence without being tied to any structured organization. It may be that one or two people were talking and expressed a need and someone said, "Let's get together and talk about that," — then others expressed similar needs and a spontaneous group was formed. Organized groups, in contrast, operate under the direction of an organization. People indicated a need but members of staff or lay leaders are the initiators. The groups then function under the direction of a group representative of all groups.

The isolated group may be a spontaneous group which exists by itself. On the other hand there will be groups which will be part of a multi-cell programme aligned with a cluster of small groups sharing common aims and goals.

Isolated single units

Contractual groups are usually for the committed Christian and have a spiritual commitment with a level of in-depth involvement, e.g. a personal growth group. The group decide to enter into a contract with each other, which involves a list of personal disciplines, to enable them to better achieve the goals they have agreed upon. Once the membership has been set they generally become a closed group for a certain period to allow uninterrupted growth. They can, by their very nature, involve a degree of threat and risk. However, it is out of this risk situation that real growth takes place. Non-contractual groups are generally for the uncommitted person. They are a more general type of group, e.g. youth cells. There is no in-depth expectations of individual members. They are non-threatening situations and open for anyone to join.

Contractual or non-contractual groups

An overview of small groups in outreach and nurture

The process of Christian outreach and nurture of new believers is a cyclical one — rather like a continuous escalator, or the recycling of a fountain. As one person becomes a Christian and begins the ongoing experience of following Jesus Christ so it must follow that that person will introduce other people to the experience. (The outward journey is based on the inward).

The central stage in this process is the individual's commitment to Jesus Christ, which willy nilly, makes that person automatically a member of a group, the whole company of Christian believers. If this commitment has taken place within a segment of that company, a local congregation or an outreach group, the new Christian will be given nurture and care. As the Christian grows in experience and love for Jesus Christ it will follow that he or she will express this love in a caring and concern for others.

Contacts will be made with friends and neighbours, friendship offered and relationships established. The Christian listens and serves and seeks to share the Good News. Through our witness and through the work of the Holy Spirit others will enter into an experience of Jesus Christ. If this process did not occur there would be very few Christians!

In his autobiography *The Seven Storey Mountain,* Thomas Merton, a Trappist monk, wrote, "When the Holy Spirit brought me to the light He worked mainly through friendships".

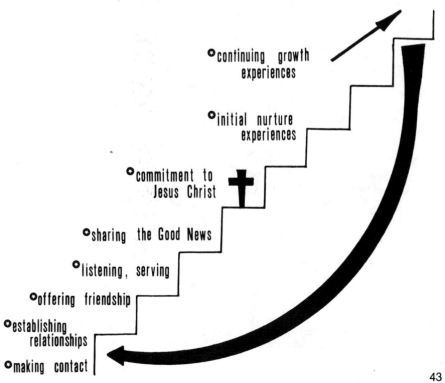

- continuing growth experiences
- initial nurture experiences
- commitment to Jesus Christ
- sharing the Good News
- listening, serving
- offering friendship
- establishing relationships
- making contact

How do we fit in small groups to the life of the local church and how do we use these small groups to reach others?

Let me introduce you to a group of people who live somewhere in south-east Asia. Most of them are young, teenagers or people in their early twenties. Their leader is perhaps older, maybe in his thirties or forties. They have come to live in X village and they have been trained for this task since they were quite young. One has responsibility for teaching the villagers the three 'R's'; another has the responsibility of helping the villagers to better health; another is working among the women to raise their understanding of their role; another is working in agriculture. The group meet regularly, often daily, for times of study and encouragement. They compare notes on their progress, and share difficulties and problems. They are totally dedicated to their work because they believe they know the way for people to follow, to help them find a better life for themselves and their country. The technical name for this group is a **cadre** and they are believers in communism.

The parallel between the Christian and the communist believer is often drawn, and the rueful comment is often made: "If only Christians could be as dedicated". As we have seen from our examination of New Testament precedents the **cadre** is not a communist invention. The principles have long been established.

Let us take "**Y**" church and community and look at it as if we were members of a **cadre** which would enter that church and community and penetrate it at all levels. The core, the basis of this penetration action would be the **koinonia** growth group or groups. This may be a group of six or more people; maybe in some situations it will be less, but ideally our **cadre** contains at least six or more people. This **koinonia** group meets weekly for a time of study, prayer and sharing. It looks outward into the church and the community and the work of the members varies.

Some may be involved in **contact groups** — on a regular or occasional basis. This contact will involve forming friendships and establishing relationships. The presentation of the Christian message may occur in the contact groups, or in **encounter (kerygma) groups** drawn from the contact groups. Kerygma means the telling forth, the announcement, the declaration or the proclamation of the Good News.

A number of members of the **cadre will** be involved in **service (diakonia) groups.** Some may be involved in educational supportive work in a **nurture (didache) group.** Didache (from which we get the word 'didactic' means instruction in the faith. From this nurture group will come people who will join or form another **koinonia** group. So, as in the steps of Christian growth, the whole process is a cyclical one. The group lives to give its life away.

Intrinsic to the whole outreach from the **koinonia group** is the prayer life of the members. In addition, there may be a **frontier support group** consisting of people who back in prayer those who are penetrating into community situations.

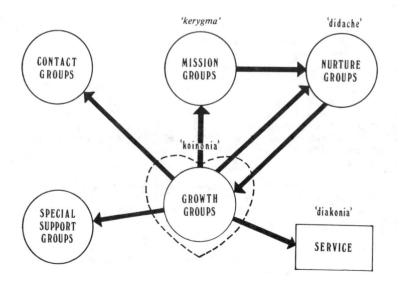

45

I would like to examine in more detail the various groups I have mentioned.

Contact Groups

These groups are a preparation for **Kergyma.** They are an important step in 'pre-evangelism' as Green calls it. Here friendship without strings is offered. The small house-centred cells allows this to take place in an informal, non-threatening, natural setting. There is also an element of ´**kerygma** present if we accept that it is not solely limited to verbalising — the life-style and action of a concerned Christian proclaims the Good News. In that sense 'contact' groups could be low-key encounter groups.

Encounter Groups

This is where **Kerygma** takes place — the telling forth, the proclaiming of the message. People are encountered in love with the Gospel of Jesus Christ. This encounter occurs in a variety of forms and degrees. The supper groups used in Lay Witness Missions or Dialogue Evangelism are examples of this type of group.

Nurture Groups

Didache involves both teaching and pastoral care. The person who responds to the Gospel in faith has only begun his Christian pilgrimage. As a new-born babe he will require our care and concern. A small group of people who embody love will provide an ideal environment in which this new life can take root, for love and acceptance is the primary need for the new Christian. This must be supplemented with teaching "by precept and example". All this will help establish him to allow growth to take place. "They met constantly to hear the apostles teach, and to share the common life, to break bread, and to pray" — Acts 2:24 (N.E.B.).

The new disciple needs support and encouragement, and this group exercises a pastoral ministry so that the new believer gains understanding in applying what he is learning to his life situation.

Growth Groups

Koinonia is a quality and depth of fellowship which can only be produced by the Holy Spirit and in which growth naturally takes place. Any Christian community should be concerned about developing vital growing Christians — people who are being brought into focus, whose steps are becoming more definite, who are being freed to live in obedience.

Growth groups are concerned with developing mature, dynamic Christian "adults". It is almost impossible for this kind of growth to occur to any real degree in a crowd. An intimate group where there is openness and honesty and where relationships develop at depth, will foster real growth.

The Growth Group is the hub of a Christian community. From it should flow care and the dynamic for evangelistic and social concern. It should be the seed-bed for personnel, for leadership and for all the actions in the name of Christ which occur in that locality. The staff for the contact, nurture and other support and service groups will and should be drawn from the **koinonia** group. This is the **cadre** of the Christian church.

Service/Action Groups

Diakonia describes the ministry of care and concern, the "servant" role of the Christian believer. Action should be a natural fruit of **koinonia.**

Frontier Support Groups

This group consists of people who back those who are penetrating into church and community situation. Some people, such as youth workers who are involved in outreach work, dealing with anti-social youth, are very vulnerable. In Newcastle, where a Newcastle Youth Service was established some years ago, the detached youth worker had two support groups to back him. One was an in-depth sharing group, whose function was to offer prayer support and a professional support group, who could give expert help when required.

A minister of a church is in an isolated situation and needs a support group.

There will be people who are attempting to offer some solutions to social injustice, who are offering Christian insights in local council, and other community situations. They are in vulnerable frontier situations in which such support groups help them clarify ideas, receive encouragement and spiritual strength and enablement.

Leadership Group

If there is more than one *Koinonia* group how do the groups and the group leaders keep in touch with each other? What or who is the link?

Leaders of each group should regularly meet together. Once the groups are truly established this need not be any more frequently than once a quarter; in the initial stages a monthly meeting may be needed.

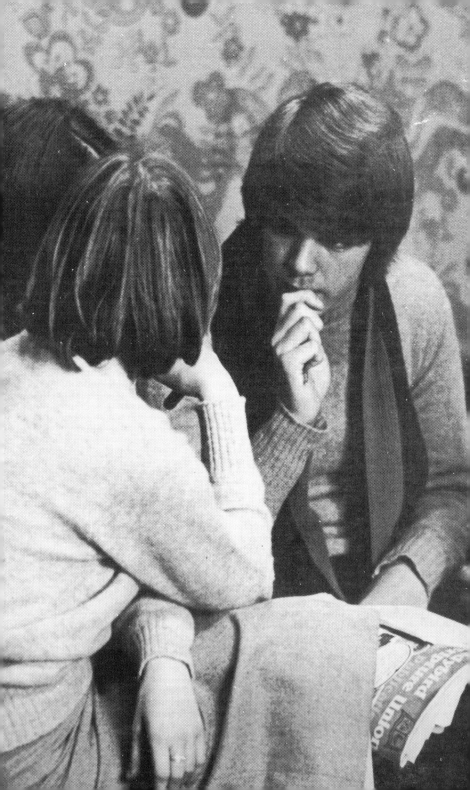

5   Guidelines for Small Groups

As we have seen, there are a wide variety of small groups. Their purpose differs according to the specific needs of the individuals involved. It is virtually impossible to give a list of guidelines which apply to all groups. In this chapter we shall consider some guidelines which apply to a number of the most common types of the small groups found within the Christian Church.

Determine the Aim of the Group

Time spent in clearly defining goals is never wasted. So many Christian groups are aimless — that does not mean they are not active — they are probably very active but they have no real direction. Groups need to take time setting their goals. This gives a clear sense of purpose and direction. A clear purpose helps reduce the anxiety and conflict which can arise where group members have different expectations. It also gives an objective criterion against which the effectiveness of the group can be measured. It gives the group a basis for evaluation.

We need to distinguish between ultimate aims or goals and immediate or action goals. The **ultimate goal** or aim expresses the long term expectations the group has for its life — the end result. The **intermediate** or **action goal** sets a clear plan of action over a specific period to achieve the ultimate goal.

For example: One afternoon you may have time on your hands so you take the family for a drive. You set off with no objective in mind. You just go for a drive! You may arrive back quite refreshed having seen a few new and interesting things or you may return quite frustrated and feeling you didn't achieve anything worthwhile, having driven up a few dead-ends.

Alternatively, as you back your car out of the drive-way, you may have a clear purpose in mind. You have to attend a 7.30 p.m. meeting at St. Stephen's Church located at the corner of Green and Red Streets, South Sydney. That represents your **ultimate** aim. However, you have never been to that Church before, therefore, to reach that location you have to look up your street directory and plot your course. Step one is to reach a particular intersection. Having reached that reference point, you then drive to a certain side street and so on. These steps represent your Action goals.

In a small group, the Ultimate goals may express the hopes of the members for a six months, twelve months or longer period. The Action goals will all be aiming towards that Ultimate goal but will cover a shorter period.

In small group conference workshops, groups spend time gaining skills in goal setting. The following is some feed-back from the workshop groups which you may wish to evaluate.

Type of Group: Spiritual Growth Group

Ultimate Goal: To become aware of our unity in Christ and express this by our love for one another.

Goals to Achieve this Aim (For first 6 weeks):
— Spend time getting acquainted with each other
— Define tasks in the group and assign to members
— Determine limits of confidentiality
— Seek to build mutual trust within the group
— Provide opportunity for sharing job situations and other experiences.

Another group expressed it this way:—

Type of Group: Outreach Group

Ultimate Goal: To promote through a sustaining group relationship the outreach of the Church.

Goals to Achieve this Aim (For first 8 weeks):
— Begin to pray as a group. To learn some skills to do this.
— Decide upon some appropriate Bible passages and plan a series of group studies.
— Begin to learn how to listen to each other in the group.
— Commence listening to others outside the group to discover expressed needs.

— Move towards open, honest sharing of our needs and joys amongst the group members.
— Seek to build new friendships with people we meet in our everyday contacts.

And another . . .

Type of Group: Contact Group (Low key outreach group)

Ultimate Goal: To win uncommitted people, including nominal Christians, to Christ using a group situation.

Goals to Achieve this Aim (For first month):
— List people who may be invited (especially lonely people).
— Decide upon a suitable location for the meetings.
— Determine the form the group should follow.
— Visit prospects and seek to establish friendships with them.

One other . . .

Type of Group: Witness Cell.

Ultimate Goal: To develop skills and confidence in sharing our faith with others and to provide support for each other as we share our faith.

Goals to Achieve this Aim (For first month):
— Determine the skills needed to be developed.
— Plan a study programme.
— Undertake exercises to begin to develop openness and sensitivity to each other.
— Draw up a brief list of group disciplines to help achieve aims.
— Begin to pray for each other daily.
— List the names of people with whom we should be sharing our faith.

> — Commence intercession for these people.
> (Keep these specific, state a clear purpose, avoid generalizations.)

Plan Optimistically

It is often the one who may seem to be the least likely person who will be interested in a group. Do not pre-judge potential interest in a group. If we have faith in people — faith in the power of God to re-create people, to produce change, then we can be optimistic about the possibilities of renewal through small groups. We ourselves need to be thoroughly convinced that small groups are a viable method for new life in the church and our enthusiasm and optimism will rub off onto other people because it is definitely contagious and you cannot get injected against it! God give us more optimists in the church today.

Train Leaders

The Christian Church does not have a good record of training people to fulfil leadership roles. Many small groups have suffered because their leaders have not been prepared for their important task. Ideally, training for leadership should take the form of basic development prior to the commencement of the group and then opportunities for "in-service" training.

Prior to each of the small group multi-cell programmes in three of the parishes in which I have served, basic leadership training was given. This varied: at Port Kembla the leadership of the groups grew out of a larger study/fellowship group which met for over two years preceding the decision to commence the small group programme. Training in the content of the Christian faith was accompanied by the demonstration of various methods of study and leadership techniques. Honesty, openness and growth in in-depth relationships were developed by experience-centred learning as participants were involved in a small group experience. Only after the small group programme was planned were these experiences reflected upon and interpreted in a structured manner. A short intense pre-service leadership development programme then sought to prepare the new leaders for their specific tasks.

On both the other occasions this small group experience for potential leaders did not precede the leadership training and for this reason I felt the leadership in some cases was not as rich as in the Port Kembla groups. This long-term preparation of a core group out of which potential leadership can emerge seems, now, to me to be the wisest way to work. However, most of us, myself included, are usually too impatient to allow for this long-term exposure to God's Spirit moulding a group and developing knowledge and understanding of the Christian message. It seems we need to begin avoiding packaged, short-term superficial training experiences wherever possible and choose the more in-depth approach.

In all our training of leaders we need to beware lest we focus purely on developing skills in group dynamics. The Christian Church is suffering today from a large overdose of the human potential movement. I would be the last to want to eliminate the development of these skills from our training, but they need to be kept in balance.

Leaders of Christian small groups need to be taught the New Testament concept of leadership. Growth in character will be seen as far more important than accomplishments. What a leader **is** is crucial. The leader's mantle is that of humility and he/she is called to lose himself in service. Distinct progress in Christian living and character which shows definite evidence of a transformation by God's Spirit is to be encouraged as essential preparation for leadership. The leader must be helped to discover that one of his major roles is to model — to be an example — a tangible expression — of the life God has called us to lead in Christ: ". . . not as being 'little tin gods' but as examples of Christian living" (1 Peter 2:3). The other major role of a leader is to teach by demonstration, by modelling, but also to impart the content of the Christian message and then to enable the group to relate this to their own life situation. The leader will also teach attitudes as well as content. The small group interaction as well as the leader's own example will provide an ideal situation for this to take place.

Example and informed, sensitive instruction will be two major roles the small group leader must be helped to develop. These cannot be nurtured to any great depth in a crash course for leaders. However, most effective Christian leaders didn't wait till they were fully prepared before they moved into leadership. They grew and developed while they led others. Groups can be reasonably effective with leaders who develop most of their small group leadership skills while doing "in service" training.

This need not only be a home — it could be an office, or a special room set aside in a church.

For most small groups it is more beneficial to meet away from the church building — partly for reasons of survival. It is possible that church centres may not be available to us — for financial reasons, for strategic reasons — in the future. We should move away from being church-building orientated while still retaining a deep sense of oneness with the total local community of faith. It is important that members feel comfortable while praying, studying and sharing. Most church facilities provide anything but an ideal situation for natural interaction between people. Take the way we have provided inflexible church seating or large halls which are difficult to either heat or cool.

The home is usually an undisturbed, intimate ambience — it has a 'family' atmosphere which is really what the group is about. In intimate, close house situations it seems easier to find security, peace, and enter into family type relationships.

Homes are also flexible. When the groups increase more homes are enlisted — when the groups decrease we are not left with expensive empty buildings to be a millstone around our necks to hold back the advance of the Kingdom.

People are apt to get confused if the meeting is held in a different home each meeting night. If they have had a roster list, they may have lost it — they may forget which home it is in and therefore they fall away. Ideally it is best to meet in the one home for a term — it may be possible to have meetings in the same home for years. It depends on the availability of the home. When choosing homes it is important not to intrude on a busy young family.

The host needs to be the sort of person who is genuinely hospitable as the wrong attitude by the host can spoil a group. People on the periphery of the church want to feel that their welcome is genuine. The people who live in the host house must be warm and friendly. The hosts and hostessses can be given some pointers — not to busy themselves with supper during the meeting, be ready on time, etc.

Supper can be useful — in that it can be a relaxing informal time and you can have some informal fellowship. However, most people are more concerned about having a well-run meeting and getting home. If there are single people they may want to stay on. The element of competition with supper can so easily creep in where somebody wants to put on a better supper than somebody else. Does

Christian fellowship always have to be linked with a sponge cake? Every time most Christians meet they want to have a banquet. There is no need to have food at all.

Determine the Size of the Group

Many ask, "What is the ideal number to have in a small group?" There is no one simple answer to that question. It depends on a number of factors — the purpose of the group and the background, maturity, sensitivity and resourcefulness of the members, along with other variables. There are some upper limits which can be set. Changes in beliefs and attitudes of persons are more likely to take place in an atmosphere of interaction between all members of the group where there is opportunity for "give and take" in the clarification and expansion of ideas.

The amount of interaction possible between people in a small group is determined by its size. There is a simple equation which expresses the number of relationships possible among people in various sized groups.

$$R = N(N - 1)$$

The number of relationships (R) equals the number of persons in the group (N), multiplied by one less than the number of persons in the group (N-1).

As shown in the diagram, when four people are involved in dialogue there is a pattern of twelve interpersonal relationships. The number increases steeply as only a few extra are added to the group.

For a group of	6	(6x5)	30 relationships
For a group of	8	(8x7)	56 relationships
For a group of	10	(10x9)	90 relationships
For a group of	12	(12x11)	132 relationships
For a group of	15	(15x14)	210 relationships
For a group of	20	(20x19)	380 relationships

It is evident that the larger the group the less possibility there is of interpersonal relationships among the participants. It is generally agreed that the upper limit for a small group in which members are able to participate meaningfully is twelve. Beyond that number the group tends to be dominated by a few aggressive members.

However, the upper limit for depth relationships is not the only factor which determines the size of the small group.

Sometimes it may be more appropriate to break the small group into sub-groups of 2 to get some quick interaction and feed-back in a plenary session on an issue or to press relationships to a greater depth. In other situations sub-groups of 3 or 4 may be more effective for particular learning experiences. For growth groups and most of the types of small groups dealt with in this book, 8 to 10 is a good number to aim at.

Twelve (or 15) not only sets the upper limit for meaningful relationships but provides a situation which is non-threatening for those who are new to small group experiences. This allows involvement of the participants to the degree they desire. It helps them exercise their individual right of dissent, to stay out of involvement in the group to any real depth without being obvious.

I always think it is significant that Jesus chose twelve men to be His close inner core group. His radical message required deep interaction with Him and each member of the group but the size of the group allowed each to determine his own level of involvement.

Often people's immediate reaction when they are asked **Don't Overlook** to join a small group is "I haven't got a spare night" and **Odd Times to** so it gives the impression the Holy Spirit only operates **Hold Meetings** between 7.30 and 9.30 on a week-night (with some variations to His schedule on Sundays!).

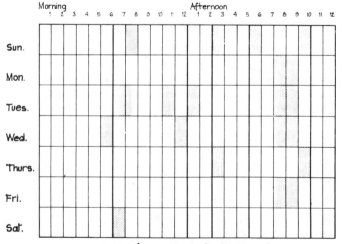

Don't overlook 'odd-times'
as possible times for meetings.

Everyone has numerous time slots in the week which are possibilities for small group meeting times. The chart dividing a week into 1 hour time slots serves to show a variety of possible times for small groups to meet. The shaded segments indicate the time slots used by groups in my parish experiences and since. Let me comment on some of the less obvious times for groups.

— A number of young mothers tried meeting during the day but were frustrated by the natural disturbance of their small children. To find quietness to study and relate at depth they chose to meet from 5 a.m. to 6.30 a.m. weekly. Not a popular time by any means but for this group, a rich growing experience eventuated which lasted for a number of years. (I am convinced a deep sense of need is the essential motivation to nudge people to consider times which are usually considered unsuitable.)

— A group of teenagers, and in another instance, businessmen, met over breakfast for their koinonia group. The host ate before the group arrived and was free to lead the group. Study and sharing took place during the meal which was always kept simple.

— A frontier youth workers' support group met at 7.30 a.m. in a regional centre where the participants did not have far to travel to work after the meeting.

— Groups of businessmen and women and tradesmen held meetings during their lunch hours. Mostly meeting in offices or committee rooms, sometimes in a corner of a workshop and one that met in a secluded greasy corner of a boiler-house!

— Students gathered for their group meetings over supper after an evening of study.

— Periods before and after church worship have been popular times for busy people.

Meet Regularly   Frequency of small group meetings will vary from group to group. Certain types of groups will need to meet more regularly than others to maintain the group life and achieve the agreed goals. However, meeting weekly generally provides the desirable frequency in most situations. Some groups will find a fortnightly meeting adequate and all that can be managed under the circumstances. Meeting more than once a week or less than bi-weekly appears to be unsatisfactory.

If a group is heavily study orientated it is helpful to meet **Meet by Terms**
by terms roughly following the pattern of school terms. In
our adult groups we generally commenced the first term
mid-February, running through to Easter week. After a two
week recess we recommenced for eight sessions till mid-
June. Third term began after a further two weeks break and
concluded prior to the August-September school vacation.
The final term ran from mid-September to late November,
closing before the heavy Advent preparations in **December.**
After running a small group programme for three years
which met for 52 weeks in the year we found this a more
sensible approach which was well received by the participants.

Meeting by terms has many advantages:

— It avoids both busy and slack periods such as Easter,
Christmas, school vacations and school and university
examinations.

— Each term a new study unit can be accomplished. This
helps hold interest and provides a range of subjects.

— The fresh start to the groups throughout the year encourages enlistment of new members who otherwise
may be reluctant to break into a group which has been
functioning for a period.

— The breaks between the terms give opportunity to make
alterations to the groups in terms of leadership or membership.

— A different home can be used for each term, providing
a variety of venues without the confusion which can arise
when a different home is used each week.

— Each term can be commenced and concluded with a
combined gathering of all the groups. The advantage of
this in preventing isolation is dealt with under another
one of these guidelines.

— The conclusion of the term provides a natural opportunity to undertake evaluation which can be overlooked
in a group which meets throughout the year.

— The period between the terms provides a welcome break
for the group without feeling guilty about missing a
meeting.

— Some leaders have used the recess to visit drop-outs
or potential members.

The term system seems to best fit the group with a
heavy study content but some other types of groups also
follow this practice. However, most growth groups usually
find it more effective to meet regularly with a recess over the
summer holiday period.

Limit the Length of Each Meeting   The length of meetings varies with the amount of time available and the work to be done. Breakfast and lunchhour groups may be limited to 45 minutes; evening groups from an hour and a half to two hours.

Regularity and punctuality are of great importance. In any effective group, faithfulness in attendance is essential. Most small group covenants list it as the first commitment the group member is asked to make. It is therefore a reasonable expectation that meetings will be held as scheduled and that they begin and close at the hours agreed upon. Other responsibilities should be respected; from keeping business appointments to getting the baby sitter home on time. Punctuality becomes a sign of the seriousness with which members regard their relation to the group. Chronic tardiness on the part of a member, or the whole group, is an indication of wavering responsibility. It could indicate resistance to the demands the group is beginning to make upon the commitment of members.

If a group is involved in an absorbing sharing or discussion period which looks like taking the group overtime, the leader should seek a group decision regarding exceeding the scheduled time for finishing.

A group-appointed time-keeper can help a group keep to the period apportioned to various segments of the programme. This person will simply act as a servant of the group and gently remind the group of the time passing. It will be for the group to finally determine its own use of the time available.

Have a Pattern for Each Meeting   Each group will need to create a particular pattern of meeting which serves its needs and situation.

There are certain elements which are common to most small groups in the Christian church: worship and praise; study — of the Bible, literature, books on the Christian faith, etc.; sharing — insights, problems, questions, judgements; prayer — of various kinds, and both silent and spoken.

A possible model which has been used is:—

— Brief worship — including praise in song and possibly some simple form of liturgy. Hymns, psalms, scripture passages and most church hymnals provide resources for simple responsive reading. One group member could be assigned the task of preparing and leading this segment.

— Brief prayer — silent or spoken to recognize the presence of Christ in the group.

— Feed-back segment in which people report on their research of issues raised in the previous meeting. Certain persons may have been assigned this task or the leader may have been wise enough not to muddle through a difficult question raised previously and now be prepared with an adequate answer. This period may also be used to recapitulate on the previous study, especially if it is part of a unit. Time may be given for sharing on the reflection of the members on the previous week's experience and how they sought to relate it to their life situations during the week.

— Study linked with discussion/sharing and hopefully some creative group work using some of the methods suggested in the companion volume to this book — *Creative Ideas for Small Groups.*

— Prayer as a response to hearing the word of God through the study period. Again *Creative Ideas for Small Groups* suggests a variety of prayer methods to use— silent, written, spoken, conversational prayer, etc. This period of prayer will focus on petition, confession and thanksgiving.

— Next may follow intercessory prayer for persons and situations raised by the group. This will be an important part of a group which has a wide vision of its mission in the world. Self centred "holy huddles" tend to neglect this aspect. It expresses a care and concern which is wider than the needs of the immediate group.

— Praise segment — this may be included at another point in the session as well as, or instead of, the conclusion. "Methodism was born in song" — but they don't have a franchise on praise — wherever God's people gather, the spirit of joyful praise should be apparent.

Make All Study Relevant

A common criticism of small groups in the church has been that they are dull, uninteresting, their studies are irrelevant and rather than produce change they reinforce limited thinking and experience. Instead of helping people grow they stunt growth. One of the reasons for this criticism is that studies undertaken in small groups have often been irrelevant. The topics studied in many cases, have not grown out of the expressed needs of the participants. The particular interests of each member have not been explored. Instead the subjects have frequently been imposed by the leader or without adequate opportunity for the group to plan together its own syllabus.

The methods of study have been another area contributing to this irrelevance and ineffectiveness. Generally, an authoritarian leadership style results in a didactic, lecture type of presentation with little or no opportunity for the group to think through the issues raised. The inductive method often has not been used. This method makes for relevance as it involves the whole group in the learning. It draws upon the individual experiences of each member, reflects upon and analyses these, and sets lines of action which will effect their life situation.

In the study of the Bible, often it has been little more than an academic or intellectual exercise. Minds have been filled with information but opportunity has not been given to apply this to where the learners are at in their personal and corporate life. The Bible is the vehicle through which God reveals His will to human kind. It is meant to foster change. It is intended to help people re-align their lives to God's intention for them in their everyday situations. Time must be taken to let this happen in other than a superficial manner. Methods, like those set out in the companion volume to this book, should be used to enable people to wrestle with the relevance of the scriptures to their inner life, their home, their work or study situation, their leisure — every aspect of their relationships. And that takes time, it involves honesty, it is somewhat risky and there will be agony of mind on occasions. But unless we make all study relevant small groups can become part of the problem rather than part of the answer.

Provide Opportunities for Worship and Communion   Instead of 30 minutes of chorus singing (which in some groups degenerates into little more than a vocal exercise!) the worship session could include some singing, a confession said by everyone, or affirmation of faith — or a poem, or a psalm, something that sets the tone for the meeting. On occasions the whole meeting could follow the pattern of a worship service — praise, confession, thanksgiving, petition, intercession interspersed with reading and study of the Word of God.

There are certain orders of service which could be adapted for small groups — an agape feast, or a Shalom meal.

"An early account of the agape meal is thought to be described in a 2nd century document called the *Didache*. The people gathered for supper and brought with them offerings of food. After this supper, the food was shared in what is now called the Mass, or communion, and the leftover food was given to the poor. Gradually the meal fell into disuse because of the problem of control, and because congregations became too large for such informal meetings . . .

Today the agape meal is becoming a popular form of worship and celebration in ecumenical church gatherings because it makes possible a form of 'breaking bread together' which is outside the confessional rules and regulations and can be celebrated by laity of all confessions."[1]

Worship Now (published by The Saint Andrew Press, Edinburgh, 1972) contains an order of service for the celebration of The Lord's Supper in a small group. It has been well received by groups in which I have been involved. It is a fairly lengthy order, but segments could be omitted without detracting overmuch.

The celebration of the sacrament has proved to be an enriching experience for combined gatherings of small groups, especially to conclude a term or yearly programme.

Avoid Isolation

Isolation can produce real problems in small group life. It is easy for a group to become inward looking and degenerate into a 'holy-huddle' or 'bless-me-club'. This is always a risk in groups with a high degree of sharing of personal thoughts, feelings and experiences, as is the case in growth groups. The high degree of subjectivity can cause the group to deteriorate unless it is balanced with more objective experiences. This can be done by introducing more objective content into group study, frequent opportunities to serve as a group and through widening the life of the group by meeting with groups having a similiar purpose.

Where it is possible, opportunities should be provided for activities with other groups. These enlarged group events help broaden the fellowship. New ideas and experiences are introduced and new leadership styles encountered.

This is reasonably simple to organize where a number of groups are involved in the same cell programme. In most of the groups in which I have been involved which operated by terms, we sought to avoid isolation in one of three ways.

— For the first meeting of the term the groups gathered together in the local church or hall to launch the term. Each group was assigned a task in the programme which varied from leading the praise segments to preparing and serving the supper. A film or specialist resource person was frequently used to introduce the theme for the term.

— Mid-way through an 8 to 10 week term, all the groups met in pairs. The leadership and venues were pre-arranged and the programme was similar to an ordinary meeting.

— At the conclusion of each term the groups converged on the local church. The programme included a sharing time in which a chosen representative of each group shared what was the most helpful aspects of the group life during the term. Also, often a panel dealt with questions raised in the groups but not answered during the term. Sometimes small group work was done in the hall with each person meeting with people other than those in their weekly group. On occasions the Lord's Supper would be celebrated together. These were enriching experiences which helped avoid the problems associated with isolation.

Small groups which are not linked with an overall programme, should be equally aware of the problem of isolation. It is useful to seek out similar groups in other denominations in the district and perhaps suggest combining for a meeting. Occasional open meetings to which neighbours and/or friends are invited will help keep the group alive. Possibly other times than those on which the groups meet may need to be considered for these special events. Times when the group as a whole becomes involved in outreach and service will also help to avoid the group becoming introspective.

The Christian church is "the servant church of the ser- **Serve to Live**
vant Lord". We are called to serve. It is not optional. It is one
of our basic characteristics. "We are saved to serve".
Where a Christian community exists for itself it soon de-
teriorates and expires. Small groups as microcosms of
Christian community must also give their life away to find it.

Contrary to the common attitude to prayer amongst
many Protestants, prayer is work. It is a way of serving the
church and the world. Protestants have traditionally tended
to regard Catholic closed orders as not being obviously
useful. Only of recent years are we discovering anew that
rich, balanced, vital prayer is one of the most important
aspects of our call to servanthood. An intercessory prayer
group which keeps its prayer life dynamic is operating
on the frontiers of service. However, such a group will
make themselves available to be a channel through which
their prayers are answered as they put legs under their
prayers to take tangible expressions of the love and concern to others.

Busy group members who are involved in their church
and community will often bypass this principle of serving to
live by asserting that they are already serving individually.
However, there is real advantage in serving as a group,
at least on occasions. Some of the richest times in groups,
for me personally, have been while working alongside
other members or reflecting together on times of group
involvement in situations of need in the community.

In one small group programme we used a regular meeting night mid-term to reach out. The groups assembled in
their usual meeting place a little earlier for a brief worship
session. The groups divided into pairs, each receiving two
or three assignments to visit shut-ins, drop outs from the
local church or those only loosely associated. They re-
grouped again at 9 p.m., shared their experiences, prayed
for those visited and had supper. All agreed these nights
were some of the highest points of the groups' activities.

This obviously applies to a situation where a number **Hold Regular**
of small groups are associated with each other in some way **Leaders**
—usually linked with a local church. The leaders' meeting **Meetings**

played a vital role in all our small group programmes. It can become a most important meeting for a number of reasons.

— It is the key to co-ordination and the maintenance of some sense of common direction. Curricula, study resources, basic and inservice training programmes, service and outreach, combined meetings and finance were all given oversight by this meeting. The leaders would pool the feed-back verbally or from questionnaires to their groups, concerning most of the above items.

— Regular evaluation was facilitated by the leaders getting together. It took place in any number of ways, informally as the leaders shared, through the discussion of each facet of the programme by means of the leaders' meeting check list, through the collation and evaluation of questionnaires distributed in the groups.

— An in-service training segment was provided in each session. Generally a chapter of a suitable book was discussed or new skills developed in brief workshops. Problems encountered in leadership were discussed and there was a sharing of ideas, skills, resources and new insights gained while leading their groups.

— It also had a clear pastoral purpose. The leaders found it to be personally supportive. Problems were shared and there was ready support and affirmation for those who shared discouragement. These leaders did not suffer from the isolation that most leaders of individual cells experience. There was always a listening ear, prayerful concern, plus training and new resources to help them in their ministry.

The pastoral aspect extended to group members. The problems of members which surfaced during the regular meetings of the group were shared in confidence, ways of providing help were discussed and they were specifically remembered in prayer. Other leaders frequently offered to provide care for the member in addition to that given by the leader of the group. Where it was reported that a member was not fitting into a group, this would be discussed and another more appropriate group found. In some leaders' meetings with which I have been involved, each group was represented by its leader and one or two members.

The degree to which stated goals are being reached **Evaluate** needs to be assessed regularly. The church is definitely not **Regularly** well known for its ability to sit down and evaluate its work. We are activists, but so infrequently ask why we are performing some function and what we are hoping to achieve. It is a new experience for most people. It is not a difficult thing to evaluate group life — there are very simple evaluation instruments available.

The chapter on evaluation deals with this in some detail and gives some practical guidelines. Evaluation by the group participants can take place either during or after the meeting, through group discussion of prepared evaluation questions, or through completion of various types of forms. When leaders gather, some worthwhile evaluation can take place.

It is also valuable to hold an annual evaluation and planning retreat for multi-cell programmes in which members and leaders participate. Evaluation forms should be completed and collated beforehand to form the basis of much of the work undertaken. The presence of a skilled resource person to help reflect upon and interpret the data adds an important dimension.

We found it beneficial, where there were a number of **Appoint an** associated groups with similar goals in a parish, to appoint **"Overseer" for** a person to act as "pastor" of these groups. The "pastor" or **Multi-Cell** "overseer" was kept free of permanent commitments as a **Programmes** leader of any one group. The "overseer's" task was to keep a finger on the pulse of the programme, act as an enabler and resource person to the leaders, convene leaders' meetings and generally administer the activity. A different group would be attended each week and the "overseer" would usually participate as a group member. Occasionally a group might be led by the "overseer" if the leader wanted to observe a new style of leadership. In some groups where there were problem members a leader appreciated seeing how another leader handled them. Consultation took place with the leader after the meeting. Although in most small group ventures in which I have been involved, this was a role played by myself (the minister), in some instances, it was effectively fulfilled by another.

Make a covenant Elizabeth O'Connor has some pertinent things to share
with each other when making comments about the place of discipline in
the Mission groups at the Church of the Saviour, Washington D.C.

> "As members of a mission group we *need to be
> disciplined* and we need to be willing to require a
> discipline of those who would be on mission with us.
> No person or group or movement has vigor and power
> unless it is disciplined. Are we willing to be disciplined
> ourselves and to require it of others when it means
> that we will be the target of the hostilities and the
> pressures of many who do not see the necessity? The
> chances that we will give in unless we know that this
> "giving in" means that our mission group will have
> no hard sharp cutting edge, and will in time peter out."[2]

Group life suffers and some groups never get off the
ground because goals and expectations of the individual
members are too diverse for the group to work together in
unity. Any healthy organization usually has a clear statement
of purpose and an agreed-upon method of pursuing that
purpose.

In forming a covenant the group will need to answer:
'What is the purpose of the group? To what discipline or
tasks will each participating member need to commit themselves to achieve the stated goals of the group? Differen-
tiation will need to be made between maintenance goals,
those which concern the life within the group and the
task goals which have to do with the work undertaken by
the group.

All covenants should be evaluated from time to time
and new ones negotiated, if necessary.

Most group covenants have these common features:
— Regular attendance
— Ordered personal devotional life
— Prayer support for each member of the group
— Practise of Christian stewardship
— Involvement in regular worship of gathered church
— Availability for service.

Louis Evans Jnr., senior pastor at **National Presbyterian Church in Washington D.C.** gives some guidelines
followed by the groups attached to his church. He stresses
they are principles and not legalisms.

"Covenant groups are an expression of our life in Christ, and cannot reach their potential unless He is an active member of the group. Our life and strength flow from Him; therefore we can take joy in His presence and express what He is accomplishing in our group as a member of it. His Word is our guide to all of life and therefore it should be used as the groups feel the need. It is out of His Word that we identify the following covenant dynamics:

1. **The covenant of Affirmation** (unconditional love, agape love). There is nothing you have done, or will do that will make me stop loving you. I may not agree with your actions, but I will love you as a person and do all I can to hold you up in God's affirming love.

2. **The covenant of Availability.**
   "Anything I have — time, energy, insight, possessions — are at your disposal if you need them. I give these to you in a priority of covenant over non-covenant demands. As part of this availability I pledge regularity of time, whether in prayer or in agreed upon meeting time.

3. **The covenant of Prayer**
   I covenant to pray for you in some regular fashion, believing that our caring Father wishes His children to pray for one another and ask Him for the blessings they need.

4. **The covenant of Openness**
   I promise to strive to become a more open person, disclosing my feelings, my struggles, my joys and my hurts to you as well as I am able. The degree to which I do so implies that I cannot make it without you, that I trust you with my needs and that I need you. This is to affirm your worth to me as a person. In other words, I need you!

5. **The covenant of Sensitivity**
   Even as I desire to be known and understood by you, I covenant to be sensitive to you and to your needs to the best of my ability. I will try to hear you, see you and feel where you are,' to draw you out of the pit of discouragement or withdrawal.

6. **The covenant of Honesty**
   I will try to 'mirror back' to you what I am hearing you say and feel. If this means risking pain for either of us I will trust our relationship enough to take that risk, realizing it is in 'speaking the truth in love, that we grow up in every way into Christ who is the Head.' I will try to express this

honesty, to 'meter it', according to what I perceive the circumstances to be.

7.   **The covenant of Confidentiality**
'I will promise to keep whatever is shared within the confines of the group in order to provide the 'permissive atmosphere' necessary for openness.'

8.   **The covenant of Accountability**
'I consider that the gifts God has given me for the common good should be liberated for your benefit. If I should discover areas of my life that are under bondage, 'hung up' or truncated by my own misdoings or by the scars inflicted by others, I will seek Christ's liberating power through my covenant partners so that I might give to you more of myself. I am accountable to you to 'become what God has designed me to be in His loving creation'." (Used with permission).

The Yokefellow Movement is a vigorous effort to give depth and direction to a full participation in the Cause of Christianity by any Christian who wishes to share the "yoke of Christ". The Yokefellow card sets the disciplines out in this way:

As one who seeks to submit his will to the will of Christ, I humbly undertake to wear His yoke in the following ways:

1.   **The Discipline of Prayer.** To pray daily, preferably in the morning with a minimum goal of 30 minutes for the devotional period.

2.   **The Discipline of Scripture.** To read, reverently and thoughtfully, every day, a portion of Scripture, following a definite plan.

3.   **The Discipline of Worship.** To participate each week in the worship, work and fellowship of a local church.

4.   **The Discipline of Money.** To give a definite portion of my annual income for the promotion of the Christian Cause.

5.   **The Discipline of Time.** To employ my time in such a way that I do not waste God's gift, but make a daily Christian witness, particularly in my regular work.

6.   **The Discipline of Study.** To develop my understanding and insight by the regular study of serious Christian books.

7.   **The Discipline of a Group Experience.** To attend weekly meetings of a Yokefellow Group, and give priority to the meetings and the daily devotional period.   69

Small groups can splinter off from a local church fellowship and become a divisive force. Frequent criticism is directed towards the small group movement for this reason. Loyalty should be a characteristic of a healthy group. This will extend to the wider Christian community of which they are a part and to its appointed leader.

Be Loyal To Your Local Church

However, I have frequently counselled frustrated and discouraged people who, having caught the vision of the possibilities of renewal through small groups at one of my conferences, have returned with high hopes and renewed enthusiasm to their local church only to have the new insights rejected out of hand by their local minister. There are a number of reasons why a minister reacts in that way. Sometimes he has experienced groups which have been badly handled and have become divisive either through a "holier than thou" attitude or poor strategy in seeking to produce change in the church. Alternatively he may be an autocratic leader who feels that unless he is running everything his authority is threatened or heresy or doctrinal unsoundness will creep into the church. There are not many like this but unfortunately some are around who dominate a church and cannot let people grow. Such a person can be destructive in a church because they have not dealt with their own personal problems, and tend to project those problems on to the group life. They are part of the reason why the New Testament concepts of mutuality of ministry, servanthood as the model for Christian leadership and authority growing out of lifestyle are so foreign to most sections of the Christian church.

Most lay people get frustrated in this situation and the groups tend to die. Alternatively if they are happy about having the minister lay down the law all the time and never question his authority or his ideas, the group may move along without change and without a great deal of vitality. It exists, it is a pleasant time of meeting, but seems to not grow or mature in any way.

We are required as Christian disciples to be faithful. Loyalty is closely aligned with faithfulness. We need to be loyal to our group, our church (its members and leaders) but above all to our Lord Jesus. If you have a small group meeting in your home it is courteous to inform the minister but you don't have to ask him to attend all the meetings, nor are you obliged to let him lead.

Divide to Multiply

We are in existence because of the biology of life—cells grow and divide and the process keeps on repeating itself. It is a basic principle of growth. Jesus taught "except the grain of wheat falls into the ground and dies it abides alone". Seeds are made to reproduce themselves by losing their own identity "dying to themselves". It is by "losing life that we find it". That is the paradox of the Christian life. If small groups want to hold rigidly to their own identity they will stagnate. Small groups, as indeed all activities of the Christian church, are called out by God to mission, to extend the kingdom and thus bring more honour to the Name of our great God and Father. The redemptive fellowship of a small group must be extended to others.

This concept needs to be taught to the group from its inception and the members should set as one of their goals that the group will ultimately reach the point where it divides in order to include others. Where this is not clearly understood the members will be threatened when it is suggested, even to the point of either closing ranks or the group disintegrating. This principle is also supported from group theory dynamics. As we saw earlier the size of the group reaches an upper limit beyond which meaningful interpersonal relationships become less possible at any depth. If a group increases to over 12 (or 15) it should divide just to ensure that it exists as a viable group, apart from the higher Christian motivation of mission.

If You Leave a Group Find or Found a Group

Once people have experienced the depth of care and concern, and growth possible in a vital small group they will generally never again be completely satisfied with trying to be a Christian alone. The small group should be aware of its continuing ministry to those who leave their groups, because they have to move out of the district. A leader with the heart of a pastor will try to find details about cells meeting in the district to which the member is moving. The group should contract together to continue to give support through prayer and personal contact.

A copy of these and other appropriate books could be given to help in the formation of a new group by the member. A sharing of resources and ideas could be offered to help the new group become established.

I have a fear in training people to lead small groups that **Depend Upon** they will depend more on the skills they develop through **Divine Grace** these learning experiences than on divine enablement. The Christian church suffers greatly today because many of its leaders depend upon their education, personality, natural gifts, business know-how and strategy more than the grace of God made available through the Holy Spirit. This is God's work we are called to, ours is to co-operate with, not replace, Him. "Without me you can do nothing" are sobering words — they speak of partnership with God the Senior partner. Our work would be more effective if we prayed more and trusted more. Our main task is to live at the centre. Our God is Sovereign of this universe, He does have clear intentions for humankind, He is able and He willingly and lovingly chooses to use the foolish of this world and provides them with His supernatural resources to bring His kingdom among men. We need to help our small group leaders grasp the relevance of this for their own leadership.

References

1. Letty M. Russell, *Ferment of Freedom* (National Board, YWCA of the U.S.A., 1972) p. 61; see pp. 59-67 for a description of a shalom meal.

2. Elizabeth O'Connor, *Call to Commitment* (Harper & Row).

6   Leadership of Small Groups

Leadership in the Church

The leadership pattern in protestant churches has been firmly established and firmly maintained for centuries. Leadership is divided between age groups and sex groups. Overall leadership tends to be by the "elders" — what sociologists call a gerontocracy — with the minister as the key leader. Even if the minister is young he tends to be in alliance with the "elders", because of church structures and patterns. If the minister tries to introduce change into a church too quickly he can find himself isolated both from the elders and from the people.

The Sunday school and the youth fellowship are traditionally the area where the younger person is permitted to exercise leadership roles. But again in many churches the general superintendent may be an older person.

Women's groups are led by women—although the president or leader may either be selected or approved by the minister. Representatives of women's groups may have a seat on the policy-making committees or parish meetings but their voices would not be dominant ones. Some women consider it wrong to speak in a predominantly male meeting or to question decisions made by the men.

Women have exerted economic power (with some behind the scenes political power). They have been pre-occupied with raising money to maintain the fabric of the church and any additions — fans, cupboards, carpets, etc. or even with paying the stipend of the minister. They have not been encouraged to assume leadership roles, except among themselves. In some churches, the traditional women's leader has been the minister's wife. During the past decade or so many ministers' wives have not accepted this job, hoping to encourage lay-leadership.

Rule by the elders has tended to mean that change has been accepted very slowly. They have not always seen their role as a teaching one, but as a conserving one. The minister, who is assumed to have had a better theological education than anyone else in the congregation is, by tradition, the teacher and is therefore frequently the only leader of study groups.

In the past the dominant role of church leaders was reinforced by an exaggerated emphasis on respect for authority. In post-New Testament times people believed that kings had a God-given right to rule and to be obeyed. Political, social and church leaders reflected the king's role. Even today some Christian writers present the leader as the person who must be unquestionably obeyed — even though that same leader must be humble about how he exercises his authority!

The world's image of the leader is that of the demagogue, the ruler, the prime minister, who authorises and ensures the enforcement of social order and law. My abridged dictionary has almost two inches of definitions of the word.

The first few meanings are:
'to conduct, to guide by the hand or showing the way, to direct the movements of;
to be in command of;
to direct or induce by persuasion, instruction or advice, etc.''

The truly great leaders and initiators are those who create, or found, or conceive something, see it get off the ground and move on in their thinking to something else. (Not all initiators are leaders; if they attempt leadership they are not necessarily good leaders). If the initiator tries to hold on to what he has created it tends to become fixed in pattern and institutionalised and so we are back where we began.

Authority

One of the problems inherent in a discussion of leadership is the question of authority. If we do not try to reconcile worldly models of authority and New Testament models there is less ambiguity. In the 1st century A.D. authority was thought of in terms of power. Christ turned this idea on its head. Jesus used the image of Himself as a servant, or as a slave. There was no one more powerless than a slave and it was unimaginable to people of the 1st century A.D. that slavery would ever cease.

Christ also compared Himself to a soldier who had to obey orders — He was under the authority of God. But this claim for authority was not reinforced by outward and visible signs of power, except in His person.

The New Testament reveals a world-as-it-was — we are in a world-that-is. In our society there is much less 'do it because I order you' — except in the armed forces, police and other services, where men are trained to cope with extra-ordinary circumstances. A soldier is however permitted to disobey orders if he considers them contrary to moral laws.

Of course there are many actions we perform without question at the request of others. A nurse assisting at an operation does not argue with the doctor about which instruments to use; a musician in an orchestra does not try to change the tempo, but obeys a conductor's guidance. In both these cases there is an element of co-operation. The nurse is a necessary co-worker with the doctor; there would be no orchestra without musicians.

The New Testament writers record Christ warning against exercising authority in the world's way:

> *"You know that in the world, rulers lord it over their sub-jects, and their great men make them feel the weight of authority; but it shall not be so with you. Among you, whoever wants to be great must be your servant, and whoever would be first must be the willing slave of all — like the Son of Man; he did not come to be served, but to serve, and to surrender his life as a ransom for many."*
>
> *(Mark 10:45)*

Lawrence O. Richards writes:

> "When we think of leadership in Christ's terms, the normal connotations must be put behind us. Leadership in the church is not related to authority: Christ only is our "leader". Christ only is the Head of His church. Leadership in the church is not related to self-aggrandisement: the leader is to be like Christ, the servant of all. In this context Paul's instructions concerning the election of church leaders can be easily understood. For a man to wear the mantle of leadership humbly, and to lose himself in service to others, his **character** will be far more important than his accomplishments."[1]

See also 1 Timothy 3:1-13.

There is no doubt that Paul spoke with, and exercised authority — perhaps he is the exception who proves the New Testament rule. His initial claim for authority was based on the fact he had seen and talked with Christ. He emphasized this when it was necessary. At other times, for example in his letter to Philemon, he said: I could order you — but I won't — I ask you to do something because of your affection for me.

The New Testament model is a person who **lives** the truth — others believe and follow. This is the key issue — credibility, integrity. Paul was so credible he was even able to say "do as I do", "copy me". If he were simply an egotist demanding adulation he would have been disregarded.

Credibility through example

Our ultimate model and example is Jesus Christ. Our credibility stems not from having "arrived" spiritually, but from a willingness to admit we have not but are still in the process of **becoming,** in the process of struggling to the goal.

Paul wrote to the Philippians:

> "*It is not to be thought that I have already achieved all this. I have not yet reached perfection but I press on, hoping to take hold of that for which Christ once took hold of me. My friends, I do not reckon myself to have got hold of it yet. All I can say is this: forgetting what is behind me, and reaching out for that which lies ahead, I press towards the goal to win the prize which is God's call to the life above, in Christ Jesus.*" *(Philippians 3:12-14, N.E.B.)*

Definitions

Perhaps leader may be the wrong word to use when we are talking about small groups. We could use the word **convenor;** or **initiator;** or **teacher** (although this implies an authoritative handing out of information); we could use the word **chairperson;** we could use the word **guide;** or **enabler;** or **fellow**-learner, **fellow**-worker, or **co-worker.** The first five words imply that one person is out front, ahead of the others; the last four imply a sharing of knowledge together.

"In fact and in short, there is an authority attaching to personal holiness which can be found nowhere else. It is the *sine qua non* of any ministry worthy of the name. He alone can exercise an authoritative ministry who often has recourse to the secret place of the Most High, who has learned to listen to the God Who speaks, who knows the meaning of obedience, who can say not merely 'I hold this view', but, 'I am held by this God'. There is something self-authenticating about the authority of a man of whom it can be said by the man in the street as it was said of Elisha by the woman of Shunem: 'I perceive that this is a holy man of God who is continually passing our way' (II Kings iv, 9).

There is nothing brash or noisy about such authority as we have just sought to describe. This is the very reverse of cocksureness. When Jesus exercised His authoritative ministry, the people were reminded of the words of Isaiah:

> *"He will not strive, He will not shout,*
> *Nor will His voice be heard in the streets.*
> *He will not snap off the broken reed,*
> *Nor snuff out the smouldering wick . . ."*
>
> *(St. Matthew xii, 19:20)*

So sensitive was His dealing with people, so reverent His handling of personality. There is no forcing of His views, no crushing of individuality." [2]

A person who chairs a meeting has to follow set or customary rules. Part of this person's authority is implicit and related to those rules. People participating in a meeting are expected to obey the rules and follow a disciplined and orderly pattern. The person who occupies the chair may have a casting vote, and ideally and customarily functions as an arbitrator, a co-ordinator and interpreter, but is not meant to control and influence the decisions of a meeting.

A guide is usually a person with a good local knowledge — for example a person who leads mountain climbers. In some under-developed countries a guide can be one rung up the status-ladder from a beggar, depending on casual jobs from tourists for a livelihood. This person is closer to a servant than a leader.

We are aiming to help people who are in existing church situations where the power-structures have not radically changed, nor are likely to change, for some time. The question of the leader's role in the church has not yet been thoroughly re-examined. In many churches lay-people have been sharing leadership (not just administrative responsibility) for a long time; in other churches this idea is still being tentatively explored.

The small group 'leader' in many churches will possibly also be the initiator or convenor of a group or groups; this person will at first possibly combine the roles of teacher and guide. This person will possibly lead the group meeting (although this is not necessary).

My preferred job-description of a small group leader is

facilitator-enabler. This implies a drawing of people together, providing resources (sometimes the leader will be a resource), encouraging people to talk and to share; creating and maintaining an atmosphere in which this is possible; enabling a situation which helps people to be self-motivated, to be prepared to discover for themselves; but above all, modelling a style of Christian discipleship, which gives the only credibility to anyone who attempts leadership.

This style of leadership involves being a fellow-learner and fellow-worker with the members of the group. It also involves sharing responsibility for the on-going existence of the group. We will discuss the concept of **shared leadership** more fully later in this chapter and describe how it works. If we imagine the group as a line of people on a bushwalk with one person as the guide and leader, we can also imagine that this person shares his/her knowledge sufficiently and shares the map so that by the time the walk is completed the job has been rotated and each group member has shared the responsibility of being leader and guide.

The Characteristics of the Christian Leader

Leadership may be your role already in your local church. Perhaps you are the person the congregation or fellowship always nominates to do the talking! Alternatively, you may have just begun to accept leadership responsibility — perhaps of a small group. Some of the people in that group — or all of them — may be relative strangers to you and you are uncertain how the group will 'click' with each other and with yourself. You may have the responsibility of preparing the framework of the discussion and you are anxious to handle the meeting in the best way possible.

We are not concerned just to educate people to become leaders who have a good understanding of group dynamics, who can move the discussion along and see the meeting finishes on time. We have first to distinguish what characteristics are inherent in the Christian leader that are not inherent in any other group leader.

John Kleinig[3] summarizes the characteristics which Paul has listed as requirements for group leadership. He points out: "except for the gift of being a 'good teacher', all of the qualities required of a leader are also expected of every Christian. They are, in fact, the fruit of the Spirit. Being above reproach, faithfulness to one's wife, sobriety and temperance, courtesy and hospitality, etc., are qualities which should be produced in the life of every Christian through the work of the Holy Spirit. The point about a leader is that his life *actually* bears these fruit: **he is a mature Christian.** Thus we can understand why leadership can be spoken of (by Paul) as an 'honourable ambition', for in large measure it is expressive of Christian maturity."

In addition to maturity a leader should "**have proved himself**", and have "**a good reputation**".

"The only special gift which Paul mentions . . . is that of teaching. A leader must be an apt or good teacher. He must have the ability and willingness to teach. This is an ability which he will recognize in himself or others will recognize in him, and of which he is a steward."[4]

"Coupled with the necessity for a leader to be a good teacher is Paul's insistence that he should teach sound doctrine."[4]

The leader as servant

The Christian leader, says Sarah Little[5] is a **redeemed Christian,** willing to make all the resources of his life available to the group . . .'

'Because this person is a Christian, his motives are not self-seeking. He sees himself as the **servant** of the group, not its master. He is willing to accept criticism, to absorb hostility, even to fail and to try again. Because his is the ministry of reconciliation, he so identifies himself with those in the group that he suffers and rejoices with and for them. His prayers for this, his visits and calls, arise from the concept of the ministry that is his.

. . . for this kind of Christian leader . . . when something real happens in a group — when a person gains a new perspective or shows courage in a decision or utters a few revealing words in a prayer at the end of a session — he knows this is not of his doing, but that he has witnessed the miracle of God at work with man, seeking him in love and confronting him with the call to discipleship.'

The concept of a leader as servant, as we have seen, is a New Testament one. It does not have quite the shock value it had in Christ's day, when Christ compared Himself to a servant.

Servant — in the passage from Mark, meant one who waited on tables. You were automatically in a lower social class if you performed a duty for someone else. (We still tend to de-value personal services.)

Christ served His disciples—He knelt down and washed their feet. This was more than a symbol or a gesture. If we relate it to group leadership a leader must care for other members of the group, must be available to them, must serve them. As leadership responsibility is shared, each group member shares in this serving responsibility.

A good small group leader is one who . . .

    . . . . sees each person as having worth and dignity in his/her own right

    . . . . respects people enough not to intrude upon their privacy

    . . . . does not force people to speak

    . . . . does not tell others to participate but creates a situation in which they can participate

    . . . . helps people to really communicate with one another

    . . . . believes each member of the group has something to say worth hearing

    . . . . is a good listener and one who encourages others not just to hear, but to listen carefully to what others are trying to say

    . . . . is patient and gently draws people out and assists them in becoming articulate

    . . . . does not manipulate the members of a group to agree with or follow his/her ideas

    . . . . is not self-seeking

    . . . . is flexible, but not casual; sensitive to the mood and expressed needs of the group

    . . . . is the servant of the people in the group and not the master

    . . . . has warmth, understanding and an easy manner

    . . . . makes all his/her life available to the group

    . . . . does not expect to be a perfect leader

    . . . . remembers a few of these fundamental guides and tries to use them as a basis.

Realization of the ideals of Christian leadership can only come from a deep relationship with God through Jesus Christ. The list of virtues might seem an impossibly daunting one, but resources are made available to us through God's Holy Spirit. The **gifts** of the Spirit **equip** us for our Christian life; the **fruits** of the Spirit are **reflected** in our Christian life.

Training for Leadership

There is a dimension to Christian leadership which differs from secular leadership. This dimension is the spiritual one and is a deeply personal thing. Paul told Timothy: 'Train yourself in godliness'. (1 Tim. 4:7). Timothy had to keep spiritually fit and his whole life had to bear out what he taught others. 'Timothy,' says one commentator,[6] 'was not naturally brave, and he was often unwell. He needed a great deal of encouragement.' Don't we all!

A Christian who assumes the responsibility of guiding and enabling others needs to be aware of the importance of 'living at the centre'. This state is achieved through a daily encounter with God primarily through prayer and the written Word. We need grace and courage to put into practice what God communicates. Christian fellowship, worship and sharing in the sacraments are also essential to personal spiritual growth.

A Leader Should Not Be

. . . . a person who takes on the job for the wrong reasons; who is on an ego trip, looking for admiration and trying to build a following. The 'personality' man or woman who counts on this to get them through the session, rather than on thorough preparation.

. . . . insensitive. Does not take the trouble to really work at developing meaningful relationships with the group. This requires real effort on the part of leaders.

. . . . 'the boss' — always directing the show. This person dominates the discussion, suppressing all that doesn't fit into his or her own ideas, experience and understanding.

. . . . disgruntled. If people have to be talked into doing the job they may find it is the right role for them after all or they may bitterly regret they allowed themselves to be persuaded into taking it on. If someone is not enjoying leadership they may be overly critical, perhaps cynical. They are not happy nor finding it fulfilling; this attitude is quickly reflected in the members of the group.

. . . . always talking. It is often the most articulate person who is chosen as a group leader; sometimes this choice is the wrong one. The person who quickly grasps the subject and is able to communicate ideas is a useful one, but is sometimes impatient of the people who are thinking more slowly. It is easier to do all the talking than do any real listening.

. . . . too casual. The group is told they are to get on with the discussion; a word of encouragement is given now and then but little or no direction.

. . . . shockable and unloving. In groups there can be pressure to conform, to say the right thing. No one has the nerve to admit they don't agree with something, or have a different idea of things in case they are howled down — or worse — considered stupid or sinful.

SOME ALTERNATIVE LEADERSHIP STYLES*

AUTHORITARIAN (Autocratic, dictatorial)	LAISSEZ-FAIRE (Permissive)	DEMOCRATIC (Group-centred, shared or functional)
1. Determines goals and policies and wants the group to choose the goal he has chosen.	1. Lets people go their own way.	1. Accepts the fact that leadership is the function of the whole group and not only of one individual.
2. More interested in the subject matter (content) than with the people (process).	2. Doesn't prepare and lets things drift.	2. Shares leadership responsibility.
3. Aggressive.	3. Doesn't seem to care.	3. Believes in other people.
4. Makes decisions regardless of other viewpoints.	4. Causes the group to accomplish very little.	4. Creates a sense of security and belonging in the group.
5. Talks too much.	5. Encourages fragmentation through indiscipline and unreliability.	5. Ensures that other members have opportunity of leadership.
6. Focusses attention on himself or herself.	6. Makes no attempt to appraise or regulate the course of events.	6. The leader's withdrawal will not mean that the group will fall apart.
7. Group members are almost puppets.	7. Lacks courage in making decisive plans.	7. All policies a matter of group discussion encouraged and assisted by leader.
8. Hostility, resistance and resentment emerge.	8. Gives little guidance.	8. Sensitive to the needs of others.
9. Discontent and aggressive attitudes among members grow.	9. Non-participation by leader.	9. Allows individual initiative and fosters personality growth.
10. Aloof from active group participation except when demonstrating.	10. Freedom of group to do as they like.	10. A group will say of a good leader who has finished, the goal achieved, "We did this ourselves".

* With acknowledgement to Geoff Waugh, who published this table in *Group Life*, a publication of the Queensland Uniting Church Department of Christian Education, Brisbane.

MAEUTIC LEADERSHIP

"There are some disadvantages and some advantages with each style mentioned above. Now for really effective, responsible leadership we should consider a style which is flexible, embracing to a certain extent all three.

This style has been called 'Maeutic' from the term 'Mid-Wife'. The role of the mid-wife is to assist at birth, giving a feeling of security, mainly standing aside and allowing natural processes to take their course, but ready to make final decisions if absolutely necessary. One could imagine an instance where the mid-wife would have to decide that the welfare of the mother may have to take precedence over that of the baby. In a similar way the Maeutic Leader is sensitive to the needs of the group, assisting in the birth of ideas and making of decisions. What is important to notice in this style is that the one in the spotlight is not the leader but the group and the event taking place.

In fulfilling the role of Maeutic leader, the leader will therefore at times need to be authoritarian, mostly democratic and even at times assume a laissez-faire style."

"The leader must have a good attitude about himself. **Self-awareness** The good leader knows his gifts."[7]

"The leader must have good attitudes about others. He must be able to see and honour the uniqueness of each person."[8]

Self-awareness grows out of our own self-evaluation, and from the constructive comments of our peers and superiors and feedback from those whom we lead. Self-evaluation involves the analysis of our feelings and actions. The reading of books on the subject is useful. An excellent book, which combines Scripture and psychology, is Cecil Osborne's *The Art of Understanding Yourself* (Zondervan). Other books written from a Christian perspective are Ross Snyder's *On Becoming Human* (Abingdon) and Elizabeth O'Connor's *Our Many Selves* (Harper and Row).

Evaluation by our 'superiors' in communication skills and/or specialist knowledge is helpful. In a small group situation an observer can be invited to sit in on the group (but not participate) and watch the group in action. The observer could be a minister or a lay-person skilled in human relations training or small group leadership who will seek to evaluate the leader's ability to maintain the group life, study content and the methods used. The observer should watch to see whether the group leader is displaying sensitivity, whether he/she is listening to people and attempting to develop relationships.

Feedback from a leader's peers is useful too. In a multi-cell programme where there are a number of leaders it should be possible to invite another leader to the group session and ask for constructive comments and criticism at the end of the meeting.

From time to time it may be useful to ask one of the group to act as observer. This person's report would be presented as the last section of a meeting. In this way members of the group can sit outside it, as it were, and watch how the group functions and interacts.

Criticism needs to be weighed up. We must be careful of being on the defensive, of automatically rejecting critical comments or of being over-sensitive and of becoming too introspective and self-critical.

If we are truly living in a Christian community — and the small group is a micro-Christian community — we need to be sharing at a deep level. A leader must be responsive and sensitive to the needs and feelings of the group. We must have some response from the group or we will feel we are functioning in a vacuum.

Human relations training

We can develop self-awareness, sensitivity to others and other leadership abilities through human relations training. This is available through most state departments of Christian Education. **Sensitivity training** courses which help people to learn to listen and become aware of other people are also available.

A leader also needs training in the area of **Group Dynamics** — in order to understand process, the needs of a group, and how to keep group life vital and dynamic.

Who is to be leader?

"And the Lord's servant must not be quarrelsome, but kindly to everyone, an apt teacher, forbearing, correcting his opponents with gentleness." (2 Tim. 2:24)

The leader of a small group can be a man or a woman. This may seem obvious but so often in mixed groups it is automatically assumed that a man will lead the group.

The leader need not be a specialist. If the leader is too advanced in Christian experience and in Biblical knowledge in comparison with the rest of the group, there could be a tendency for the group to sit back and listen, let the leader cover all the ground and give all the answers. The leader does not need to know every subject well. When necessary a 'resource person' can be invited to the group; someone who has a wider knowledge of the area under examination. This person could come in either at the beginning or end of a study series.

The leader should have some obvious qualifications for the job.

Hopefully a group leader will be able to communicate easily, with a gift of making a subject interesting and alive. No one should be afraid of leading a group. You may feel inadequate — you may feel you have not many gifts useful for leadership. But if you have been asked to take on the job of leader someone has discerned that you have something to offer! Perhaps that quality is an ability to be really interested in people. Leadership is something which can be developed; both our natural and spiritual gifts can be enlarged and matured.

In the small group most of us begin on a more or less equal level. If it is primarily a prayer group there is not one who is going to claim to be a better pray-er than the others! But there will be people whose conversation and prayers reveal insights that the Holy Spirit has given to them. It is likely the group will want to share these insights and hence one person or two people may take the role of leader. **Sharing leadership**

Where a group is primarily a study group, if the study programme follows a book, or a series of lectures or notes, the need may be basically for a convenor and chairman, with the occasional contribution of a resource-person.

Shared leadership is not a radical concept. Paul spoke about his fellow workers early in his ministry, in his letter to the Romans. He also spoke of them in the church at Philippi. Paul was admittedly a person who spoke with great authority; but he was in a unique, unrepeatable position as a receiver and an interpreter of totally new doctrines.

He trained other people to be resource-people, group leaders and overall directors of small group programmes.

We have to find the median between anarchy where no one will accept or be a leader (in theory) and authoritarianism where one person, and one person only, takes leadership responsibility. We have already discussed the problems and implications of leadership at length because they need assessment. In some groups it is possible that responsibility for the continuance of the group and its work is shared so satisfactorily that no one person is leader. This may be considered an impossible ideal (or idyllic) situation.

Frequently in church groups we tend to assume that only a few people would be competent, or have sufficient knowledge, or are sufficiently mature to handle group leadership. We tend to forget that 85 per cent of a church member's life is spent earning a living, or running a home efficiently, or both. That person has to be competent or out of a job.

Sharing leadership does not mean reducing knowledge and competence down to the lowest common denominator but rather helping a group achieve a higher level than they have previously known. If the leader of our hypothetical bushwalk (p. 78) scaled down his teaching or kept back some of his knowledge, or hid the map, the group would soon get bushed or go over the cliff.

We must avoid what Charles M. Olsen calls the 'Big Daddy' style of leadership. He says: 'The church and the world call for leaders who stand alongside the people, not above. The new leader struggles to help people discover for themselves where God leads rather than issuing pronouncements from a removed position. He asks: "Who are you? What do you want to become? What are your gifts?" He enables persons to discover their identity and God's call; then he helps them to express their call in ministry.'[8]

There may be those in a group who will become dependent on the group leader—particularly in a growth group or a group for new Christians. In these groups a leader is a guide with a very great responsibility. It is possible that one or two members of the group will lean on this person, model their actions, even their lives on that of the leader, indulge in some hero-worship and feel that if the leader ceased to be in charge of the group they could not cope with things.

A leader of such groups has to be aware of the dangers as well as the privileges and joys. 'It is not I, but Christ' has to be real, has to be true. A leader is not indispensable — a good leader should be able to step out of a group and the group should continue to function satisfactorily.

Paul in his letter to the Corinthian church stresses a 'mutuality of ministry' . . .

Mutuality of ministry

> *"Now there are varieties of gifts, but the same Spirit; and there are varieties of service, but the same Lord; and there are varieties of working, but it is the same God who inspires them all in every one. To each is given the manifestation of the Spirit for the common good."*
> *(1 Cor. 12:4-7 N.E.B.)*

Sharing responsibility and leadership does not mean merely to delegate some of the tasks and lighten the leader's role, but to truly recognize that we all have spiritual gifts. Paul's model of the church as 'a body' is found in microcosm in a small group. The group is a team, each member has unique experiences, skills and special gifts to contribute. A true small group leader sets up the situation to facilitate this growth towards the New Testament model of 'a body' with only one Head (Christ) and all the members working together, caring, supporting and ministering to each other.

> *'One man . . . has the gift of wise speech, while another . . . can put the deepest knowledge into words'.*
> *(1 Cor. 12:8 N.E.B.)*

Group leaders should try people or offer people varying tasks, for, as we fulfil a different role, we offer a different aspect of ourselves.

Every Christian disciple, no matter how seemingly insignificant that person may be, has spiritual gifts. The Body of Christ is the poorer when these gifts are not shared with the faith community. The gifts are not just manual or intellectual skills, but are spiritual gifts.

Every group leader must work to put themselves out of the job. We must be aware of emerging leadership in the group. Some members will respond more quickly than others — revealing more sensitivity and understanding, developing skills in leadership. A group leader watches for people who have obvious qualities for leadership.

A Group-Centred Leader, will display some of these characteristics in his or her relationship with the group:—

- Will accept the fact that leadership is the function of the whole group and not only of an individual.
- Will share leadership responsibilities with others in the group according to their abilities.
- Will believe in other people.
- Will help create a sense of security and belonging to the group that others will be encouraged to participate and share.
- Will be aware that there are forces within the group which can enable the group to help itself.
- Will seek to ensure that other members have the opportunity of leadership.
- Will endeavour to contribute in such a way that his/her withdrawal will not mean that the group will fall apart.

The leadership team   The small group should not be run like a business meeting or be too rigid in structure. The assignment of tasks is done in an informal manner and the jobs are rotated among members of the group.

Here is an example of shared leadership in a Bible study group.

The team drawn from the group could consist of:

— Leader (or presenter)
— Blackboard Member (or Flip Chart Controller).
— Recorder (or Reporter).
— Researcher
— Time Keeper.
— Observer (occasional).

From outside the group is drawn:

— Resource persons.
— Observer (or Evaluator).

The team who share leadership do not usurp the role of leader, but are back-up people, a support group.

Let us take for example a Bible study group and see how members of the group fulfil their tasks.

The leader opens in prayer (or asks another group member to do so) and gives a brief introduction of the material. Perhaps it is an epistle of Paul. Some of the blackboard material (headings, etc.) has been prepared beforehand, or has been put on flip charts; there may be other applicable visual aids.

The leader may then go on to briefly give the background to the particular epistle the group is studying. Different members of the group are asked to read the chapter, section by section. Perhaps it falls into three obvious divisions and each division is taken by itself to be studied.

One of the members may have been asked to do some **research** on an aspect of the study and he gives his findings. (The resources pooled for this group include a handbook of the Bible (e.g. the new *Lion Handbook of the Bible* published by Scripture Union (Anzea publishers in Australia); a concordance, a couple of paperback commentaries (e.g. William Barclay, William Neil's *One Bible Commentary*, the Scripture Union series, the Tyndale series), or larger commentaries such as I.V.F. *Bible Commentary*, the *Interpreter's Bible*, a paperback on doctrine; A Bible Atlas may be borrowed from a library or minister. In addition a Bible translation with notes, such as the *Revised Standard Version* and the *Jerusalem Bible* are in the reference 'pool'. A number of modern translations are also to hand.

(It is worthwhile checking your public lending library for Christian resource books. There are quite often some useful books in the religion section. Books in the history section can be useful for background material — e.g. books on Israel or on Roman history).

The blackboard member is the servant of the group, the right hand of the leader. The blackboard member is asked by the leader to note particular points as the discussion proceeds. Sometimes the blackboard member will take the initiative and note something down; the leader may be asked to check it; 'Is this what we are getting at?'

The role of the blackboard member should not be confused with that of the recorder. The recorder concentrates hard on making a summary of the key points, but the blackboard member helps to visualise the thoughts of the group. Key points are not forgotten as the group gets involved in the discussion; the blackboard too is a useful means of clarifying these points.

One point may have to be re-written a number of times until the group feels that it expresses clearly what they are trying to say. The blackboard member may write up the point, members may discuss it, amend and develop it, and it is rewritten into a final form.

The blackboard can be used for visualising a group formulation, (or summary). The formulation may be done by the leader and written up on the board. The leader asks the group to examine the formulation and check whether it expresses what they are saying. One member may suggest the alteration of some words or ask for a segment to be restated in another way. If it is on the board it enables people to think more clearly.

The recorder is most commonly used in a conference setting or where there is to be only one meeting. Following the presentation of the lecture or study the meeting breaks up into 'buzz groups', one member of each group being a recorder. The recorder does not try to keep a full account of the discussion but notes the key points and new insights.

The recorder should check with the group leader if he is uncertain about any of the points he has noted. He prepares a summary which is then contributed, usually verbally, to the plenary session. A good recorder can summarise the discussion in an interesting way. If another group has come up with much the same ideas the recorder will be flexible enough to adjust his report, rather than reiterating these points again.

In a continuing group the recorder's role could be extended so that he or she functions as a secretary, if necessary, and lists members present, the place, the time and the subject of the meeting. In addition, a report or summary of the meeting could be prepared as a permanent record; perhaps kept in conjunction with a record of prayer requests and prayer 'experiments'. There is no need for the same person to retain the role of recorder at every session.

The timekeeper's job is an unobtrusive one and varies, depending on the type of group. Gentle reminders of how the time is moving and being spent are given. The timekeeper is perhaps most useful in a conference session, or a sharing group.

If there is a set number of questions to be answered

in a discussion, it is the job of the timekeeper to work out how long the group can spend on each one. After the discussion of the first question the timekeeper could break into the conversation to indicate to the leader that the group have spent, for example, five minutes on the question. The leader could then ask the group if they want to spend more time on discussing it or move on to another question.

As with all the other members of the leadership team, the timekeeper must be aware that he is not trying to direct the discussion.

In a fellowship group the timekeeper's role is rather limited. The leader can indicate at the beginning of a meeting how much time has been allotted for each segment of the meeting. It may be necessary for the timekeeper to point out that the time allowed for, say, the sharing session has run out, and the leader — or the leader and the group together — can decide to keep going or conclude the session. A timekeeper should not be too rigid about keeping time, but sensitive to moods and how things are going. We cannot ration the Holy Spirit to so many minutes of a meeting.

The observer from within the group is asked by the leader not to participate for a particular session and to watch the group at work. Like the visiting observer (see below) this person sits outside the group and does not participate. This should be an occasional exercise only — a 'pulse-taking' of the group.

Every member of the group should be given the opportunity to fulfil these roles. Obviously there will be members to whom we will allot certain roles on certain occasions because they have natural gifts and are able to do the job satisfactorily.

The person with poor handwriting may not make a good blackboard member and the person who does not think very clearly may not be a suitable person for the recorder's job on an important occasion. Some people find it very hard to comprehend verbal discussion. You will not know what people can or cannot do until you have tried them out.

The wider team
Occasionally the leader may invite a **resource person** to visit the group. This person may be a Biblical or theological specialist for example or someone who has made a study of a particular subject.

The **observer (or evaluator)** may, as has been noted, be another leader, a minister or a layperson, who may, at the leader's request, or as part of an overall group programme plan, visit a group from time to time to see how it is functioning. The observer is not an inspector, but aims to help the group and the leader understand their progress and development.

The observer does not participate and does not normally sit within the group. The group inter-play is observed — how frequently various people speak, how freely the discussion moves. A flow chart may be used. The observer notes whether one or two members monopolise the conversation, when things go off the track or when the discussion gets bogged down. The observer is as objective as possible in his assessment and comments.

The observer's assessment can be used in two ways. The events of the meeting may be recapitulated with the leader alone after the group has dispersed or an evaluation can be presented to the whole group at the end of the meeting.

The value of an evaluation presented to the whole group is that it focuses their thinking on how the group handled the discussion; how some members were really in agreement, saying the same thing in different ways. 'Did anybody think of . . .'? 'Why do you think you discussed . . . when it really wasn't relevant to the subject'?

The role of the observer is discussed more fully in Chapter 12, "Evaluating Small Groups".

Leadership techniques

a. **Question making** — this is the tool the leader uses in order to stimulate talk and contributions from all members.

Occasionally a question may be directed at an individual to draw him out, or to get a hearing for a shy member who obviously wants to break in. What do you think of this idea?

The general use of the question is to throw it out to the whole group — like throwing a ball into the centre of the ring for anyone to catch.

Straight questions should be used — not those which are weighted in one way or another such as "Don't you think . . .?" or "You don't think, do you . . .?"

The leader learns not to answer most questions which

are asked but re-directs them to the group as a whole or occasionally to a specific person.

Questions to the whole group can even be used to move the meeting along to a new phase of discussion, or to create any other necessary activity. When a person is dominating a discussion a question to that person or to the group or another member can re-direct the discussion. When the time set for the group has expired but there still could be extra time if required (e.g. in a conference setting), a question can test whether the group wishes to conclude or pursue the discussion further. Any summary can be tested to see whether the group agree it represents their feelings.

b.   **Re-statement.**

Discussion often gets bogged down because people don't comprehend what others are really saying. Either there is poor listening or the speaker does not express himself clearly.

The leader re-states to check that contributions are being received clearly — "Am I right in understanding that this is the point you are making?" or "Are you saying this?" Sometimes a matter needs to be expressed in different terms or more fully or in clearer form.

c.   **Articulation of a group formulation.**

In groups which are seeking answers to a particular problem it will be necessary for the leader to summarise a point to give the group an opportunity to move along to the next issue. The leader gives an outline of what he/she understands to be the group's conclusion and then gives a further brief opportunity for approval or amendment.

Sometimes there will be the sudden realisation that the main discussion part of the meeting is almost over and no solution has been reached. If this happens the leader should say something along the line of "We have just so many more minutes out of what we have been saying here. What have we agreed on so far?"

The use of silences

Brief lulls are no reflection on the adequacy of a leader. Leaders should learn not to "jump the gun" by breaking silences too soon. They are a most valuable part of the group process. The members are usually silent because they are thinking or within the silence members can be motivated to think. Before the leader cuts in with a question ample time is given to the group to break the silence themselves.

The flow of discussion   The leader interferes with the discussion as little as possible letting it flow back and forth within the group. The leader is not the "chairman" of the meeting, therefore the members do not have to address "the chair". Unlike formal meetings one member does not have to address another "through you, Mr Chairman . . .". It neither routes through the leader nor is dependent on the leader's permission.

As has already been pointed out, this does not prevent the leader from cutting in if the group is in difficulties.

Discussion should be like this . . .
(enabling, functional, leadership).

(laissez-faire).
Not like this . . .

Nor like this
(authoritarian).

References:

1. Lawrence O. Richards, *A New Face for the Church* (Zondervan, Grand Rapids, 1970), pp. 112-3.
2. The Archbishop of York, The Most Rev. F. D. Coggan, in "Religion and the Church" in *Authority in a Changing Society,* Ed. C. O. Rhodes (Constable, London, 1969), pp. 32-33. Dr. Coggan in this article is primarily concerned with the role of the clergyman but there are many insights which are relevant to our discussion.
3. John Kleinig, *The Group, Its Nature and Role* (ANZEA, Sydney, 1974), pp. 22-3.
4. ibid, p. 24.
5. Sara Little, *Learning Together in the Christian Fellowship* (John Knox Press, Virginia, 1956), pp. 79-80.
6. Donald Guthrie in *The Lion Handbook to the Bible* (ANZEA Publishers).
7. Charles M. Olsen, *The Base Church, Creating Community Through Multiple Forms* (Forum House, Atlanta, 1973), p. 117.
8. *The Base Church*, p. 118.

An Ideal Group

At least two people who are love-givers — affectionate, affirming, confident of God's love and able to convey it to other people.

At least two people who are alive to the world around them — who know what is happening in the outside world, who are concerned about issues like conservation, poverty, discrimination against coloured people, migrants and women.

At least one non-conformist — somewhat of a devil's advocate — who can bring another viewpoint. Who can empathize with another person's position — who doesn't see everything in black and white.

At least one person who is steeped in the Bible — not to reel it off pat — but who can bring penetrating points from the Scriptures to the group life and discussion.

At least one person who has a rich, deep prayer life. Who can share this with the group — who encourages the group to prayer experimentation; who has a feeling for liturgy as well as for informality.

At least one musician — be it singer, or piano, or guitar or record player. Who can share musical delights and happenings; who can enrich the group life with new ways of worship and praise.

At least one person who is creative and can lead the group out of dull, lifeless ways into new and exciting methods of learning, praying and serving.

At least two people who are serious about growing and seeking, who are prepared to explore together the implications of the lordship of Christ in every area of their lives.

At least two people who are prepared to risk being open and honest with each other, who will throw away their masks in search of authenticity, credibility and integrity.

At least one person who is hospitable; whose home is always open as a meeting place for the group, and whose door is open to any who wish to drop in uninvited in search of a listening ear.

At least a number of people who will embody some of these attributes within a group of 10 or 12.

7 Understanding and Helping Members of Small Groups

Groups are for people

'It is . . . within the church that a person might hope to experience koinonia, that fellowship, that sense of community binding Christians together — a fellowship which is, indeed, far more than a sense of "groupness". Baillie says that God's eternal purpose for man was that he might be a part of this fellowship, and that, through the fellowship, he might become what God intended him to be.'[1]

Every group is made up of people and each one brings into the group experience, attitudes, prejudices and needs. If a sense of real fellowship is generated members of a group will want each other's help and advice. Worries, fears and doubts can be brought out into the open in an atmosphere of loving acceptance.

The **so**-efficient person may admit a feeling of inadequacy; the apparently warm person a feeling of hostility. The atmosphere of the group should be such that people will feel free to express their feelings. Anger, fear and dislike are better brought to the surface and dealt with rather than bottled up. The leader needs to assure the group that it is O.K. to be openly angry rather than piously pretending conflict is not present. Face it and deal with it in the group, don't try to put a cap on it. Conflict can draw a group close together as new levels of openness and love are reached.

We need to guard against over-simplifying people's problems, of giving superficial answers. If we are to help people we must really listen and be sensitive to pick up nuances, the feelings underlying what we are saying. We must be ready too to admit that we don't always have an answer to every problem. We must then function as bridges between the problems and some specialized person who may have the answer.

A leader may have to deal with extravagant statements or a tendency to exhibitionism from a member. If we are particularly enthusiastic about something we may test our thoughts out on it in the group but we must not push a 'line'.

One of the most thrilling things that can happen to a group, as it becomes established and as masks are allowed to drop, is that God uses these times of closeness. As we share other people's hopes and fears, as we pray for each other, our spiritual and human discernment grows. You may find the group seeking each other out, apart from the meeting times, as it becomes a truly sharing-caring fellowship.

If practical help is offered this involves genuinely being available to people when they want us, not just when it is convenient for us.

Group needs are three in number—

(i)   The need for a task.
(ii) The need of the individual members.
(iii) The need for group maintenance.

Group needs

Every group must have goals with (usually) intermediate aims. The **task** overlies the aim. If the interest and commitment of the members is to be maintained and their imagination captured everyone needs to know what this task is and the consensus must be that it is worthwhile.

For example, a small group may form with a vague idea that it will be both a study and service group. Somewhere along the line the service idea may dissipate and some members may become very restless and dissatisfied. "We are always studying and never doing", they may say and they may drift away or openly rebel. If there is a profound misunderstanding about the aim or function of a group from the outset then the group is doomed to dissolution.

Each member brings to the group situation their sum of their life experience to that point — their conditioning, their attitudes, prejudices, points of view. **Each one brings their needs as people to the group.** These needs are not always admitted and may range from a basic insecurity to a constitutional inability to sit still on a hard chair in a small room!

They may have a need for recognition, for status, acceptance, to belong, to do something worthwhile. These needs do not have a direct bearing on the task of the group (unless it is specifically a growth group). They do have an influence on the group as it works at its task. These individual needs must be recognized and accepted; they will inevitably affect a person's participation and task achievement. *"To understand people, I must try to hear what they are not saying, what they perhaps will never be able to say."*[2]

The group may be hindered and there may be little advance in the personal growth of members if they become totally absorbed in the task process. Behaviour patterns may also "screen" the person from the group — for example the person who must always be clowning. The group may accept this *persona* and the role becomes more exaggerated. The person playing a role may be unhappy about it—for once having accepted a role everyone is expected to maintain that role. The unhappiness may be expressed in general dissatisfaction with the way the group is functioning. A group leader may be split in trying to deal with the disharmony and dissatisfaction between people in a group or trying to push on to fulfil the group task.

Group maintenance is concerned with the need to preserve the group life. While the group is comprised of individuals each is brought together in community for a common purpose. The life of the group needs to be kept free and healthy for it to retain its unity. Every member is committed to the maintenance of the group.

Keeping a balance between these needs

For the group to operate in a way which will bring fulfillment to the members and achieve the purposes for which it exists, the leader and the members **will need to keep these three needs in balance.** There will be times when the task will be seen to be dominating the group to the exclusion of the needs of individual members or the total welfare of the group. At such times the group will need to pause to become more sensitive to each other. People matter more than goals or tasks. But on the other hand, a group pre-occupied with the need of an individual member can bog down with its over concern and result in anguish and frustration because it is not achieving its purpose. This will be especially so in a task oriented group such as a planning committee. A balance has to be held between the tension of the fulfillment of the group task, the fulfillment of individual need and the maintaining of oneness within the group as a whole.

To ensure maintenance we have to be aware of our **The roles** responsibility to the group function. We may fulfil one or **people play** several roles in the group.

(i) Maintenance roles — roles which serve to keep the group functioning as a group and only indirectly lead to the accomplishment of the task of the group.
(ii) Task roles — roles which directly aid the group in the accomplishment of goals or in the solution of problems.
(iii) Individual roles — roles which satisfy individual needs but often hinder group progress.
(iv) Supportive roles — roles which tend to be sensitive to other members of the group in the expression of their individual needs.

These roles are not performed consistently nor are they necessarily performed at the same time. There will be change, overlapping; they will occur at different times in the same group.

Every group is comprised of a variety of individuals who will bring their own personalities, attitudes, values and behaviour to bear upon the group. Each will play different roles in the group. Not all of those listed below will be found in the same group (hopefully!). Others are more fully described later in this chapter.

1. **Harmonizer**
   a. Attempts to reconcile disagreements.
   b. Minimizes conflicts.
   c. A "Let us all be friends" approach reduces tension.

2. **Blocker**
   a. Interferes with progress of group.
   b. Keeps group from getting its work done.
   c. Goes off on a tangent.
   d. Reacts negatively to all suggestions.
   e. Cites personal experiences unrelated to problems.

3. **Flier**
   a. Won't, can't deal with situation.
   b. Avoids confrontation.
   c. Changes subject.

4. Helper-Facilitator
   a. Opens communication by encouraging others.
   b. Is warm and friendly — making it possible for others to make a contribution to the group.
   c. Clarifies issues.

5. Intellectualizer
   a. Puts discussion on a high plane.
   b. Gives little lectures on theories.
   c. Talks about "Basic Concepts" or "It is known that".

6. Non-participant
   a. Acts indifferent or passive.
   b. Doodler — daydreams.
   c. Withdraws from group by using excessive formality or verbally perhaps by whispering to others.

7. Learner
   a. Relies on authority or sanction of others — "My lecturer says that", or "Research indicates that".

8. Fighter
   a. Aggressive.
   b. Works for status by blaming others.
   c. Deflating ego of others.
   d. Shows hostility against group or some individual.

9. Initiator
   a. Suggests new ideas.
   b. Proposes solutions.
   c. New attack on problem.
   d. Definitive approach.
   e. Organizes materials.

10. Joker
   a. Clowns.
   b. Jokes.
   c. Mimics others.
   d. Disrupts work of group.

11. Dominator
   a. Interrupts others.
   b. Launches on long monologues.
   c. Tries to assert authority.
   d. Dogmatic.

In terms of the group needs, we have already considered it may help to be aware of the function of the above roles within the group. The "Harmonizer" or "Helper-Facilitator" will serve to keep the group functioning as a group, thus maintaining the group life. The group will be aided in the accomplishment of its task by the "Initiator" and the "Helper-Facilitator". The "Flier", "Fighter", "Joker", "Blocker" may hinder the group progress as they seek to have their individual needs met. However, sometimes they can perform a useful function in drawing the group together to cope with the demands they make upon the group or force the group to re-examination or exploration of new directions.

Helping 'problem members'

"And above all these put on love, which binds everything in perfect harmony. And let the peace of Christ rule in your hearts, to which indeed you were called in the one body. And be thankful.
"Let the word of Christ dwell in you richly, as you teach and admonish one another in all wisdom . . ." (Colossians 3:14-16).

It is all too easy to categorize and pigeon-hole people who do not see things our way as 'difficult' or 'problems'. It is essential we do not rely on first impressions nor cast people into stereotyped roles. We must be wary of projecting our own hang-ups on to other people. We may feel inadequate in one person's presence or we may feel superior to others who don't conform and fit into the pattern **we** want. On the other hand, you may not meet many problem people in your groups.

When a group has been established for some time the basic difficulties or awkwardness of group interaction will have been sorted out. The leader is able to deal in a relaxed manner with situations as they arise. The leader can say to a chronic interrupter: 'Ron, we know you're keen to chip in here, but just give Bev or Geoff a go for a while'. Or, to a very rigid person: 'Yes, Susan, I can see what you mean, but shall we discuss it a bit longer and see what other people think?'

After a period some people may feel that they would like to join another group. If the group meets by terms then the end of the term would be the logical time for a re-shuffle and exchange of members. In a conference situation where a group is working well together, they may be most reluctant to break up and form new groups.

Some people may leave the group in anger or frustration. They may not be compatible with the group and sometimes it will be right not to attempt to persuade that person to rejoin that particular group. We all have what John Powell calls "ego-defense mechanisms". These ego-defenses are compensations cultivated to counterbalance and camouflage something else in us which we consider a defect or a handicap."[3]

The last line of John Powell's book — 'Sorry, but that is the way I am . . . I was like this in the beginning, am now, and ever shall be . . .' is a handy motto and delusion to have around you if you don't want to grow up."

Our growth, the growth of the group, will depend on our willingness to grow, to change. On the other hand, John Powell warns: "We must be very careful, extremely careful, in fact, that we do not assume the vocation of acquainting others with their delusions. We are all tempted to unmask others, to smash their defenses, to leave them naked and blinking in the light of the illumination provided by our exposure. It could be tragic in its results. If the psychological pieces come unglued, who will pick them up and put poor Humpty Dumpty Human Being together again? Will you? Can you?"[4]

There are times when we feel we must speak. It can be devastating to find that members of a group with whom we have shared deep fellowship are fundamentally in disagreement with us on important issues. They may have made their judgments on the basis of misinformation or misunderstanding. If we know this to be the case we can quietly share our knowledge of the true facts with them. We may feel so disturbed that we feel there is no point continuing our fellowship together. "If Mary feels like that about 'x' what must she think about 'y'? I imagine it's on the same lines." The other person may think we are equally misguided! We have to be able to say: "I cannot agree with you . . . but I respect and love you". Tolerance means being able to listen and accept a person even though you may be at opposite ends of the pole on some issues. Many of the greatest Christians had "blind spots". These are obvious to us, as Christ said, even though we cannot see our own large areas of miscomprehension.

We are all potential "problem" group members. At times we may reveal aspects of the mythical people described in the following pages. This is not a do-it-yourself psychology kit, and there are not always instant cures for the problems. Very occasionally a person may approach or join a group and may reveal very definite need for psychiatric treatment or care. When someone or something is too hard to handle within the group you will have to involve other people (say a minister or an elder). There are some Christians who feel all nervous or mental illness can be cured by referring a person to the Scriptures. For some this may be true but we must, as part of our caring for others, guide anyone who needs help to someone who can treat their condition.

Let me introduce you to:

- **'Marty Luther'** (or 'Here I stand and I'm not going to budge'). This person sometimes combines dogmatism with a deprecating manner and says: 'I know you are all more intelligent and better-educated than I am, but I've always believed that . . .'' He feels threatened if a different interpretation of a Bible passage is put forward. Not necessarily a literalist or 'fundamentalist', often a traditionalist. Tends to dismiss Biblical scholarship — or any scholarship for that matter — as something nasty. (Often a graduate of the 'school of life'). 'My mind's made up — don't confuse me with the facts' is inherent in his attitude. A devastating habit is to say in a pious voice at the end of a discussion: ''Well, I'll pray for you . . .'. If this person has been particularly involved in a discussion don't ask them to close in prayer — you'll all end up with spiritual egg on your face!

For this person everything is in black and white and there is no room for doubt. You must accept 'Marty Luther' where he is and as he is and love him. You are not going to convince him by bludgeoning him with arguments, no matter how persuasive. You are entitled to express your own feelings about the issue, but without hostility. If this person attacks other people in the group because of their views you must mediate.

If 'Marty Luther' can let go a little he can be a valuable member of the group because of his knowledge and background. If he is growing he *will* let go a little. Don't put him on the outside.

- **'Chattering Charlie'**
  Often interesting, but never stops. Sometimes a supreme egoist, sometimes a bore. Often the life of the party, but trivia and great issues are both treated alike. Suffers from the 'Look at me' syndrome. (Has cousins 'Whispering Wilma' and 'Wisecrack Willie' [or 'Clarrie the Clown']).

This person must accept the discipline of the group and this must be established from the start. It has been suggested that the chatterer's constant talking is indicative of other problems in that person's life. Perhaps the chatterer's gift of confidence and articulateness could be used by having him present some material as part of a study.

- **'Dominating Dorothy'** is first cousin to the chatterers. She has to be the boss — has the most urgent, and to her, clearest views. She dominates with her voice. Her mind is often first-class but she lacks manners. She may be aware of this tendency to dominate but she may need help to control it. If she is not aware she has to be told.

The positive, good things she contributes to the group should be recognized, then it should be quietly pointed out that her impatience with slower thinkers is obvious and that she must not stop other people having their say.

- **'Silent Sam'** is the opposite type to the dominating talkers. Never a peep from beginning to end of the session. If you are feeling a bit unsure of yourself this can be worrying. Is he bored? Is he feeling it's all a waste of time? Is he really shy? Is he getting anything out of the group at all?

We often undervalue silence. It does not always mean non-participation. Some people like to get a total understanding of the issues before launching into a discussion. This is a quality to be valued.

Silence **can** mean total misunderstanding. It can also mean shyness and insecurity. It can mean true humility and modesty. If you try to force the quiet people to participate they may withdraw even further. They must be accepted as they are and must also realise they are wanted. If possible from time to time chat to the quiet one after the group session to see how things are with him. This person, as he becomes confident of the group, will share. You can ask the quiet man for his opinion on what is being discussed, but avoid obviously putting him 'on the spot'.

- **'Negative Norm'**

'I said to him, "Wilbur Wright," I said, "You'll never get that plane up in the air".' (Old joke).

A negative person is often very hard to take. Their way of getting attention is to go against the tide. They are common in church organizations, alas, and are sometimes real stirrers and trouble-makers. Their negating of everything is often a cry for help. In practical matters they may be first-class, but very often one-man-shows; they've alienated all the potential help. They are usually the people who, after everything has been decided, try to undo the decision. Their negative views are often coupled with a belittling attitude and perhaps an attempt at manipulation. Attempting to suppress them all the time won't work — let them have the floor — but be on guard.

The negative people can be confronted head-on when they have hurt another group member, and be rebuked. (But remember — we speak the truth in love). Like many bullies this may help them realise just what they are doing — at the time. They may apologise effusively and then do the same thing at the next meeting.

The leader may have to tackle this person directly and say: "What is worrying you? You seem so unhappy about how things are done in the group". In church situations we often let 'Negative Norm' get away with it — because we don't want to upset anyone. When confronted, the negative people are likely to flounce away in a huff — but they usually come back. They need us too. Forgiveness has to be related to a loving discipline.

The negative ones need our love and acceptance. Change is not going to come overnight — it may take months, years. Don't get into a huddle and discuss this person. Accept the positive contributions — and let the negative statements come out, without the group feeling hostility. Try to help the person see what is happening.

- **'Peace at any Price' Paul** (or **the conformist**). Paul can't stand controversy of any sort — and particularly in the church context. He can save the day on occasions but often construes argument as disagreement. He gets very worried if two members of the group engage in vehement discussion. He has to interfere: "We don't want to get too hot under the collar".

He has to learn that a question has to be resolved if possible and putting it aside will not do this.

- **I-Irene'** may, if she is feeling like it, say 'Good evening'. She can be infuriating and worrying because she seems turned off, not interested. If she's in the mood she is a valuable member of the group, but often her mind is on higher things and she lets this be known. She can be very off-putting to new Christians as she may seem to cut them dead or be barely tolerant of them. She will often not turn up to the group meetings because she 'has other (better?) things to do'. She is suffering from a bad dose of superiority complex; is frequently downright rude.

This problem has to be dealt with on a person-to-person basis. She must be told how apparently rude she is to other people — and how upsetting.

- **'Prickly Pete'** gets very worked up about some things, but won't recognise it as anger. His feelings may be expressed in hostility, quiet withdrawal (at simmering point), sarcasm, criticism or rudeness.

Anger in other people (and in ourselves) is disturbing and we usually try to smooth it down. There are going to be times when people get angry — these occasions can be very stimulating and will promote growth, if the stimulation is handled properly. It is not wrong to express our emotions when we are feeling deeply. If Pete **constantly** expresses his anger he really is a problem. Can he be helped to recognize the reason for his hostility and how sustained it is? If he understands why he has a general feeling of hostility he may be halfway to healing.

Direct confrontation sometimes pays: "What's got into you tonight?" Let Pete have his say. If one group member is angry with another and will admit it, don't let the whole group side one way or another; see if it can be sorted out by the two protagonists, then let the group weigh in to discuss the problem. If mature people will admit their hostility they are half-way to healing. (This is not an excuse for self-indulgence).

- **'But' says Bill** . . . and he takes us back to what we talked about fifteen minutes before; or to a sermon he heard ten years ago which had a story about . . . He has a tendency to break up the flow of discussion — particularly if he's feeling uncomfortable about the subject under discussion.

It is no good howling him down with 'But, we've been through all that'. If it is a genuine misunderstanding recapitulate briefly and see if it can be cleared up. If you feel a person has deliberately changed the subject, you could ask why he or she did so.

We must be firm in dealing with problem people for the sake of the whole group, but we must not be ruthless. As we noted earlier, occasionally someone will turn up with whom we are just not equipped to deal and we must seek help, and specialized guidance. It is not wise to try and deal with this person yourself; be prepared to discuss the problem with another leader, or your minister, or a counsellor, or a psychologist or a specialist in group dynamics. One person should not be allowed to destroy group life.

Much of a leader's handling of these situations will occur outside the group sessions in a personal counselling relation. The confidentiality of this counselling is essential.

Nine problem people have been listed — stereotypes. Where are the **normal** people of our groups? We are dealing with people who have the same psychological needs (although in different degrees) and people with spiritual needs. Each of the 'problem' people need the group and what it offers and the group needs them. If the group is going to grow it has to learn to accept these people. Excluding them may not necessarily ensure a better group. No matter how high our ideals and aims for the group we must not manipulate it and organise it to **our** satisfaction.

We are not trying to mould everyone to our way of thinking or into a group of people indistinguishable from one another.

If we are truly growing in Christ then some of the problems will diminish. You cannot expect every group meeting to be a happy experience for every member. Growth involves effort, discipline and pain. Sometimes our growing will be taking place in stress situations.

Paul's letter to the Philippians embodies the thoughts of an ideal leader. Notice how he yearns over his people, how affectionate he feels towards them and what he expects of them.

> 'So if there is any encouragement in Christ, any incentive of love, and participation in the Spirit, any affection and sympathy, complete my joy by being of the same mind, having the same love, being in full accord and of one mind. Do nothing from selfishness or conceit, but in humility count others better than yourselves.

> 'Let each of you look not only to his own interests, but also to the interests of others. Have this mind among yourselves, which you have in Christ Jesus who, though he was in the form of God, did not count equality with God a thing to be grasped, but emptied himself taking the form of a servant (or slave), being born in the likeness of men. And being found in human form he humbled himself and became obedient unto death, even death on a cross.' (Phil. 2:1-8).

If this work is to be 'sanctified by the Holy Spirit', if people are to meet God in the group, to grow into Jesus Christ and to learn His Mind, then the group must be receptive to the Holy Spirit and understand His work. ('. . . be transformed by the renewal of your mind' [Romans 12:2]). The Holy Spirit is God's agent of growth and change in human beings at all levels of spiritual life — collective and individual.

Pointers

- Don't typecast (putting people into boxes).

- Don't project your own problems in assessing others (e.g. sense of inadequacy).

- First impressions are not always valid.

- People can grow and change for the better — a sensitive group can be an agent of change.

- Abnormal behaviour is a symptom which has a cause — We need to spend time with people — to know, to understand, to help.

References:

1. Sara K. Little, *Learning Together in the Christian Fellowship* (John Knox Richmond, Va., 1956, p. 18).
2. John Powell, S.J., *Why am i afraid to tell you who i am?* (Argus, 1969), p. 113.
3. *Why am i afraid to tell you who i am?* p. 103.
4. *Why am i afraid to tell you who i am?* p. 117.

8 The Role of the Holy Spirit in the Christian Fellowship

Gordon Dicker

Relationship between the Holy Spirit and Christ

If we are to speak in a Christian way about the Holy Spirit we must proceed with caution. In the first place we must note carefully how the New Testament speaks about the Holy Spirit, and especially how it describes the relationship between the Holy Spirit and Jesus Christ. That relationship is pictured in at least three ways, two of which are important for our topic.

(1) Jesus is the sender of the Holy Spirit. This relationship is set out very clearly in the Fourth Gospel. "If I do not go, your Advocate will not come, whereas if I go, I will send him to you" (Jn. 16:7). In line with this, the Holy Spirit is often represented as the Spirit of Jesus Christ. "God has sent into our hearts the Spirit of his Son" (Gal. 4:6); "The Spirit of Jesus Christ is given me for support" (Phil. 1:19). Also in keeping with this understanding of the relationship it is emphasised that the work of the Spirit is not a new work, but the completion of the work of Christ for humankind. John's Gospel says: "He will not speak on his own authority . . . He will glorify me, for he will take what is mine and declare it to you." (16:13-14). Thus the work of the Spirit is closely tied to the historic, once-for-all work of Jesus Christ. He takes what was there and then accomplished and applies it to us, so that it becomes an operative reality in our lives here and now. So it takes place that the revelation in Jesus Christ becomes a revelation **to us** and the salvation accomplished in Jesus Christ becomes **our redemption.** In other words, the fact that we here and now share in the grace of the Lord Jesus Christ is the work of the Holy Spirit.

(2) The Holy Spirit is the presence of the risen, exalted Lord. There are numerous passages in the New Testament where an identity is suggested between the Spirit and the presence of the risen Lord Jesus Christ. For example, in John 14:18, speaking of the sending of the Spirit, Jesus says: "I will not leave you desolate; I will come to you." In 2 Cor. 3:17, Paul writes: "Now the Lord is the Spirit."

Of course, the identification of the Spirit with the exalted Christ cannot be made complete, but insofar as it goes, it makes it possible for us to speak of a new, freer work of the Holy Spirit which is something more than the making real of the once-for-all work of the incarnate Christ. In contemplating this role of the Holy Spirit some caution is necessary. The person and work of the Holy Spirit must never be totally separated from the incarnate Christ, for the risen Lord who is present in the world in the Spirit is none other than the risen Christ of whom the Gospels speak. So there cannot be any conflict between the free work of the Spirit and the teaching of Jesus. Nevertheless, this way of understanding the Spirit does enable us to recognise many more aspects of the Spirit's work. One such work would be the gift of assurance (Rom. 8:16). Another work of Spirit is the bestowing of the **charismata**, or gifts, which are spoken of in 1 Cor. 12-14, Romans 12 and Ephesians 4. Paul makes it very clear that these gifts are not bestowed on us for our own personal gratification; they are given to equip us for carrying out Christ's mission in the world, for building up the body of Christ and for the edification of our fellow members. Because this is the aim of the Spirit's work it should be clear that it is not just an individualistic work. The well-ordered life of the church is as much the work of the Spirit as the redemption and edification of the indivdual (1 Cor. 14:39-40); (Phil. 2:1-2).

From what has already been said it should be inferred that the Holy Spirit is personal. If the exalted Christ is present in the Spirit, then the Spirit cannot be thought of as just a "power", an influence or a quantitative "something" of which we may have a greater or lesser amount. It is true that sometimes, especially in the Old Testament, the Spirit is spoken of in an impersonal way, or likened to impersonal things, such as water, just as Jesus likened himself to a door and a vine, but this must not cause us to think about the Holy Spirit in an impersonal way.

The close relationship between Christ and the Spirit which has been described earlier, should warn us against thinking of the Holy Spirit as **a third** God. Christians believe that God is one, not three. Certainly the doctrine of the Trinity speaks of God in "three Persons", but the word "Person" is open to misunderstanding today because of the way in which the meaning of that word has changed. It would perhaps be better for us to speak of God's three ways of being God. The Holy Spirit is one of God's ways of being

God. He is God as God meets us here and now in the midst of our human existence in the world.

At the same time we must be careful not to think of the Holy Spirit as just a part of God, as though God were an object that could be divided in thirds. The One who meets us as Holy Spirit is not less than God in all the fullness of His being. Thus in the Holy Spirit not only do we meet the risen, exalted Lord and share in His grace, but through Him also the love of God is poured out in our hearts (Rom. 5:5).

The meaning of "fellowship"

Let us look now at the word "fellowship". Perhaps we feel that we know quite well what it means. Certainly it is a common word and is not confined to church circles. "The meeting begins at 8 p.m.," says the notice, "but come at seven-thirty for fellowship." Human beings are made for community and togetherness. To be sure there are the few odd "loners" but they are the exceptions, and mostly they appear to us to be odd. But of course, it is not just common human togetherness we are interested in. What we are enquiring about is something special, namely that extraordinary fellowship that is spoken of, and sometimes reflected in, the New Testament. What is it really?

It may surprise us to find that in one way it is not really different from what is commonly understood as fellowship. The Greek word commonly rendered as fellowship is *koinonia*. It is derived ultimately from the word *koinos*, which means common. This is the word used in Acts 2:44, where it is said that those who believed "had all things in common". So a *koinonos* is a person who has something in common with another, a partner or sharer, and *koinonia* literally means the state of sharing, of being partners, of having common or mutual interests. When it is all boiled down, that is what all fellowship is: sharing together in some common object.

There are some things we all share in common. We share with all people a common humanity and we all participate together in a common human predicament. On that basis many fellowships spring up, in the pub or club, in an army unit preparing for battle or on a cruise ship touring the Pacific. With some people we share more specific things such as nationality, race, class, religion, work and hobbies. These things also may be the basis of numerous fellowships. They may also be barriers to fellowship. We may find it impossible to have fellowship with people of a different race, class or religion. Yet with those with whom we share some of these things we may have fellowship that is meaningful and lasting.

Christian fellowship also is based on sharing things in common. What distinguishes it from all other fellowship is the nature of what is shared by Christians. If we try to state all that Christians share in common we shall have to make a very long list. For example, they share together in the Gospel and in a common response to it; they participate in one baptism and share one holy meal; they look to one holy Scripture as sufficient rule of faith and life and they have one hope of salvation. However, the New Testament speaks particularly of three things shared in common by all Christians; They are all partakers of Christ; They are all partakers of God's love and they are all partakers of the Spirit.

We may not often think of our relationship to Christ in terms of "participation", or "sharing in" Christ, but this is in fact a common New Testament way of describing that relationship. The Epistle to the Hebrews describes a two-way sharing. He shared our human nature in order that we might share in his divine life. "The children of a family share the same flesh and blood; and so he too shared ours . . ." (2.14 N.E.B.). The end result of his sharing in our condition is that "we have been given a share in Christ . . ." (3:14 N.E.B. Margin). We are familiar with Paul's use of the metaphor of the body of which all Christians are members. That metaphor is developed in numerous ways and for various purposes, but the basic idea in the doctrine of the Body of Christ is that all faithful people share together a single life in Christ. The same idea is conveyed in the Gospel of John by the metaphor of the vine and the branches (John 15). Through baptism we have a share in Christ's death and resurrection (Rom. 6). We are also called to share in his sufferings here, with the promise that we shall share in his glory hereafter (Rom. 8:17). Above all, and by way of summary, it must be said that we share in the grace of the Lord Jesus Christ. Because of this sharing in Christ, earthly distinctions no longer count for anything: "There is neither Jew nor Greek, there is neither slave nor free, there is neither male nor female; for you are all one in Christ Jesus." (Gal. 3:28).

That Christians share in God's love is so obvious that it hardly needs to be stated. The whole point of Christ's death is that it is both an outworking of that love and a demonstration of it. "But Christ died for us while we were yet sinners, and that is God's own proof of his love towards us." (Rom. 5:8 N.E.B.). The aspect of *sharing* in God's love comes out especially in those passages which speak of us as adopted sons (Gal. 4: 4-7; Rom. 8:14-16). John draws the inference of this very clearly when he writes: "See what love the Father has given us, that we should be called children of God . . ." (1 Jn. 3:1), and of course, this in turn implies that we all are brethren and ought to love one another.

If we ask how it is that we come to participate in Christ and share in the love of God, the answer of the New Testament is that it is through the Holy Spirit. As we noted earlier, Christ is not simply a figure of history, but in the Spirit he is present and active amongst his people, creating the body in which they participate, and of which he is the head. "By one Spirit we were all baptized into one body . . ." (1 Cor. 12:13). So also it is through the Spirit that we share in God's love. "God's love has been poured into our hearts through the Holy Spirit which has been given to us." (Rom. 5:5). Of course, in the first instance it was through the death of Christ on the Cross that God's love was mediated, but it remained distant and uncomprehended until the outpouring of the Spirit at Pentecost. Today also the meaning of Calvary remains hidden from us apart from the gift of the Spirit. It is through the Spirit that we discover that we are sons and daughters of God and by the same Spirit that we make our response: "Abba, Father".

The gift of the Spirit

In view of what has just been said, it is not surprising that, according to the Book of Acts, the gift of the Spirit was the primary and most important thing shared in common by all Christians. The amazing community described at the end of chapter 2, which even expressed itself in sharing of all possessions, was the direct outcome of the event of Pentecost. This was not just an exciting experience, but the reception of the Spirit as a gift permanently shared. One can judge how essential that gift was from the words of Paul: "If anyone does not have the Spirit of Christ, he does not belong to him" (Rom. 8:9). The gift of the Holy Spirit is the hallmark of the Christian, and hence the gift of the Spirit to Cornelius settled absolutely the question of his baptism. (Acts 10).

Of special interest is the concluding verse of 2 Corinthians, so familiar to us all: "The grace of the Lord Jesus Christ and the love of God and the fellowship of the Holy Spirit be with you all". But what is the meaning of the phrase "the fellowship of the Holy Spirit?" The grace of the Lord Jesus Christ is the grace which He imparts; the love of God is the love He pours out on us. One might assume therefore that the fellowship of the Holy Spirit is the fellowship He creates and gives to us. Perhaps this is the understanding behind the N.E.B. translation: "fellowship **in** the Holy Spirit". However, after careful study of Greek usage and other contextual matters, L. S. Thornton[1] believes the correct translation should be "the participation (or, sharing) in the Holy Spirit". In other words he believes the benediction points to the three most important things which Christians share: the grace of Christ, the love of God and the gift of the Holy Spirit. However, the other meaning cannot be absolutely ruled out, and is not out of harmony with this meaning, for it is precisely the participation in the Spirit that creates the Christian fellowship. This is the point that must be given the fullest emphasis: fellowship arises from sharing things in common; what makes Christian fellowship distinctive and different from all other fellowships is the nature of what is shared, and that pre-eminently is the gift of the Spirit.

It is not too much to say that until, within any group of people, there is a deep awareness that what holds them together is nothing less than the sharing in this one gift of the Spirit, their fellowship is not, strictly speaking, a Christian fellowship. Sooner or later this will become apparent when someone of different social or racial origin tries to join the group. Then subtle, and not so subtle, pressures to exclude the person will indicate that what holds this group together is not sharing in the Holy Spirit, but sharing in some social or racial class, or some other common factor. If the fellowship is truly constituted by sharing in the Holy Spirit it will not depend on bonds of this kind, whether conscious or unconscious.

As well as creating fellowship by being the object shared, the Holy Spirit has also a more active role in creating and sustaining fellowship. Fellowship is always in danger of being disrupted by human sin. Even those who are justified by grace through faith still have sin remaining in them. Their selfishness and self-centredness must be broken again and again if they are not to offend one another, or be offended. This also is the work of the Spirit.

The Spirit creates and maintains fellowship

The active work of the Spirit in creating and maintaining *koinonia* is underlined in 1 Cor. 12, where it is made clear that it is the Spirit who makes of many members one body in Christ. "for by one Spirit we were baptized into one body . . . and all were made to drink of one Spirit" (12:13). We possibly have here a reference to the two sacraments, baptism and holy communion, and the inference is that insofar as they are efficacious it is through the working of the Holy Spirit in each, creating and sustaining the fellowship of the body of Christ.

However, it may also be, as Thornton suggests, that here, as in many parts of the Scripture, the Spirit is likened to water, in which one is baptized, and of which one is made to drink. What is more, the word rendered "drink" here is also frequently meant "to irrigate". So we might also find another set of metaphors in this verse. At the beginning we have the picture of the convert undergoing baptism, and then in the second part the picture of a piece of dry land being saturated with water. So the Spirit of God penetrates to the depths of our being, like water drenching the ground. If we use our imagination a little further, it is not hard to see here a picture of how the Spirit integrates the many members into one body. Dry earth can never be moulded together into a single entity. It immediately crumbles apart into dust, whereas wet soil clings together.

In the natural state Jew and Greek, bond and free would not hold together. Jealousy and rivalry stemming from diversity of gifts can even disrupt the fellowship of Christians unless these ugly reactions are extinguished by the Spirit. "The Go-Between God" is the name John Taylor[2] gives to the Holy Spirit, because the Spirit is God going between the individual and his neighbour, making them aware and sensitive to each other, so that at the point where they meet they are bonded together in fellowship. A fellowship will only remain a Christian fellowship as its members remain open to this "go-between" work of the Spirit.

References: 1. L. S. Thornton: *The Common Life in the Body of Christ* (Dacre Press, 1950), p. 69 f.
2. John V. Taylor: *The Go-Between God* (S.C.M. Press, 1973).

9   Keeping Group Life Vital

Small groups have a crucial role to play in the renewal of individuals and society. All the liberating forces of the small group, now recognized by the social sciences, have been inherent from the beginning in the church. When the divine power of the Holy Spirit present in individuals operates in conjunction with the natural power of group relationships, people can be set free to relate to each other and to God in new and deeper ways.

Relationships within the small group are the most important factor. Whatever the purpose of the group, what happens to the people involved is more important than group structure or work accomplished.

The group itself does not cause spiritual renewal. But the structure and the dynamics of a small group seeking God's leadership provide an atmosphere conducive to growth, discovery of gifts, commitment and service. **Renewal is a gift which God in His grace bestows upon those who genuinely seek Him.** This is important to keep before us throughout this chapter. While drawing upon the insights of group dynamics, as a Christian group we must always be aware of the additional Factor present in each group. Technical know-how provides the framework in which the Holy Spirit may or may not choose to work renewal.

The dynamics of the group

Groups are more than just a certain number of individuals together; more than just the sum total of their membership. In every group, whenever people come together, unique emotional pressures are at work. These pressures arise from the different relationships within the group, the group's relation to the outside world, and the different needs individuals bring to the group. These forces and pressures help shape the nature of each group. The feeling of "team spirit" is released when a group is committed to a particular goal and to some extent to each other. But these forces are not only constructive. People will often change their behaviour or do things that they would not normally do as individuals when in a group. We refer to these forces as "group dynamics".

One of these forces is known as **"group cohesion"**. This refers to those pressures which encourage the members to join and maintain their membership of the group. The individual will relate to a group to the degree that he sees it meeting some of his needs. And the extent to which the group can meet these needs of its different members will determine the degree of group cohesion. Leaders should be aware of the most common needs individuals bring to the group for satisfaction:

— A sense of belonging and love

— A sense of purpose and meaning.

— Be able to share in planning.

— Have a clear understanding of what is expected of themselves and of the group (i.e. the group's goal).

— Experience genuine responsibility and challenge.

— Feel that progress is being made towards set goals; a sense of achievement.

— An intense desire to be kept informed.

— A desire for recognition when it is due.

— A reasonable degree of security.

In addition to the positive forces (sometimes called **"rewards"**) listed above which encourage group cohesiveness ,there are forces working **("dis-rewards")** against membership also at work. Some of these could include:—

— A loss of free time.

— The presence of "problem" members in the group.

— Ineffective leadership.

— Lack of opportunity to 'do their own thing'.

— Destructive competition among the group members.

While these may appear obvious, we often tend to think of a group from our own rather than the other member's point of view. Although we cannot make our groups appeal to everyone we should be aware of the effects of both the rewards and dis-rewards from the members', or potential members', point of view.

People bring their own assumptions, attitudes, mental sets, values, etc., to the group. Feelings and prejudices are communicated through words, intonations, facial expressions, posture, etc. Be sure that you are at least aware of your own attitudes and feelings as they affect the group's life, for you can be sure that they will be communicated, either verbally or non-verbally to the group and will affect the meaning the other members draw out.

It is also necessary for the leader to be aware of the **"informal organisation"** within the group, i.e. the values, relationships, etc. that may not be provided for by the official, formal group structure and organization. The nature of the informal organization within your group will depend on how your group sees itself and its purpose. (This is one reason why goal clarification and periodic evaluation of the group life and task achievement is so important.)

If your group is primarily "task-oriented" (i.e. concerned above all with the achievement of the observable objective — e.g. planning a particular project), the informal organization will favour those who are productive and helpful; if companionship oriented, then those who are companionable and friendly. However, to be really effective groups need to be efficient in performing their task as well as effective in their interpersonal relationships.

Informal organization involves the aspect of **informal leadership.** The informal leader is the leader(s) in practice in the group who are not provided for by the formal group structure. The informal leader furthers the real interest of the group; his behaviour comes closest to the group ideal — he is the group representative. Such a person may not necessarily be appointed *official* leader of the group. It is important then to recognize your informal leaders — don't feel threatened by them. It's not necessary to formally incorporate them into the leadership team but it is essential to utilize them as a communication channel to the group. Recognize them as an asset and relate to them accordingly. Have them on side!

Proper and effective **communication** is the most strategic factor in motivating a group. But communication only takes place when the meaning (i.e. the facts plus the subjective interpretation of the facts) *intended* by communicator coincides with the meaning *interpreted* by the group. For this to happen communication must be seen as a two way process. The communicator (leader) must listen to the group as well as talk. Indeed speaking and listening skills should be used to build a warm, accepting, friendly climate in which all members feel free to participate in relevant communication and discussion. The flow of communication is affected by the interpersonal relationships within the group and the relevance of information being communicated to the life and purpose of the group. For upward communication (i.e. from the group to the leader) to take place the group must be provided with a supportive and accepting climate. As has already been indicated the leader, through his knowledge of group dynamics, but **more** importantly through his love and concern for the members of his group, must facilitate this climate.

It should firstly be stressed here that as Christians we are not in the business of manipulating people to either our views or the lifestyle we might believe they should follow. However, groups are concerned with the learning, growth and development of its individual members, and therefore we should be concerned with **helping people change and grow.** To influence the behaviour of individuals in a group we need to deal with the group as a unit, because the individual is held in position by forces pressuring him to conform to the group's standards. So you need to "unfreeze" the existing group standard through uninhibited discussion, free expression of views and feelings and perhaps changing the physical environment (e.g. a more relaxed physical setting), until the group as a whole accepts a higher standard. As Kurt Lewin, one of the leaders in the field of group dynamics has said, "It is easier to change the ideology and social practice of a small group handled together than of single individuals."

It is important then for group leaders to be aware of the forces below the surface in their groups and to be able to, in some degree, manage them. Jesus Himself understood the importance of group dynamics and to some extent utilized those forces in His ministry. In the small group of 12 disciples ideas, attitudes and behaviour were changed. Group dynamics is a very real tool that the Holy Spirit uses to minister to us and through us to each other.

The presence of God in our relationships

The amazing thing about a small group in the church is that it does not battle along on its own innate resources alone. Christ, our Lord is there too! And part of the group experience is to look beyond the group and consciously acknowledge and value His liberating, strong presence. (Some groups set aside an extra chair as a symbol of His presence with the group.) Then His thoughts and His en-abling come to be highly valued as they "come alive" in the Bible, in prayer, and in the Holy Spirit speaking through the insights of others in the group. **His** touch is felt. So the group not only becomes aware of the human limitations of its members, but it also experiences the reality of Jesus meeting needs in an experience of power. Each person in the group focuses on who Jesus is and what He is doing in each life. The Living Word brings the presence of God into the group relationships.

Factors which affect our communication with others

There are at least five major factors which contribute to the way in which a person is a good communicator or a poor communicator — a person's self-image, listening, clarity of expression, hostility and the degree to which a person is prepared to reveal him/her self.

1. Self-image

When speaking of our self-image we are speaking of the concept we have of ourselves "Who am I?"; "How do

125

I see myself and my situation?" "For what do I stand?"; "Where am I in life?"; "What are my values?"; "My goals?"; "What do I believe?"; "Who influences me?"; "Am I inferior?". It may be said our self-image is the very centre of our being from which we see, hear, evaluate and understand everything else.

It is important to see the way our self-image affects our communication with others. A healthy, strong self-image is necessary for vital and satisfying interaction with others. It is the concept of the person who has come to an acceptance of themselves physically, emotionally, and intellectually. This person has recognized their good attributes as well as acknowledging lesser ones, and sees that there is a higher potential toward which all can grow, but is aware that that vision needs to be a realistic one. This person will recognize that every individual is different, with various capabilities and talents; that each person is affected to a tremendous degree by past experiences, particularly from childhood and adolescence, but will recognize too the supreme worth and importance of every human being; and that within each person is the capacity for change and growth. A person with a healthy self-image lives fully and confidently, enjoying life and people.

A person with a poor self-image is insecure, lacks self assurance, is over concerned for what other people think, feels unworthy and inadequate. Because of this he/she feels that his ideas and thoughts are uninteresting and are not worth communicating. This person fears rejection, criticism and so has difficulty in relating to others in an open, honest way. "I am afraid to tell you who I am, because if I tell you who I am, you may not like who I am, and it's all that I have." ["Why am i afraid to tell you who i am" — by John Powell S.J., (Argus Communications, 1969) p. 12]. John Powell continues by saying, "this thought reflects something of the imprisoning fears and self-doubt which cripple most of us and keep us from forward movement on the road to maturity, happiness, and true love."

As we have seen, our self-image comes in part from our childhood, and our conditioning. Cecil Osborne writes:

"We need not be forever the victims of all our earlier conditioning. We can change. We are not the blind victims of either heredity or environment, with no power to alter our destinies. There is a divine inner capacity which enables us to be more than we are. It is important, however, that we do not deceive ourselves, and that we recognize the deeper inner feelings planted there long ago, and which still reside within. Why bother? Simply because self-honesty is essential to honesty with God. We cannot know God any better than we are willing to know ourselves. If we are afraid of our own deep inner feelings, we will to the same degree fear God, though even this fear may be repudiated and buried deeply with other emotions."[1]

He continues: When we become ". . . willing to have God's best for us, when we no longer fear His will but seek it as the supreme good for our lives, we can believe what God already believes about us — that we can be vastly more than we are. We can come to have a new self-image and act in harmony with that new concept."[1]

As our self-image affects the way we communicate, so our communication with others shapes our concepts and the way we see ourselves. We derive a great deal of self-knowledge from our experiences with other human beings, particularly from the "significant others" in our lives — parents, family, peer group, and those we love. Are we liked or disliked; acceptable or unacceptable; worthy of respect or contempt, a success or a failure? If a person is to have a strong self-image he or she needs the assurance of the love, respect and acceptance of those who are the "significant others" in his or her life. It may be that in a supportive small group a member may have these needs met in a way which will enable **growth** and acceptance of themselves which has never previously been possible.

2. Listening

Listening doesn't only mean the physical process of hearing with the ears — it involves an intellectual and emotional process as well, when one's whole being strives to understand and hear the thoughts, feelings and meanings behind the words being uttered. It requires patience, sensitivity, understanding, acceptance and alertness.

Carl R. Rogers, in a paper entitled "Some Elements of Effective Interpersonal Communication" points out the need for people to be heard. When bursting with insoluble problems, going round in tormented circles, overcome by feelings of worthlessness and despair, we need an individual to rescue us from the chaos of our feelings. These individuals need to hear without judging us, diagnosing, appraising or evaluating us. They need to just listen, clarify and respond to us at the levels at which we are communicating.

"I can testify that when you are in a psychological distress and someone really hears you without passing judgment on you, without trying to take responsibility for, without trying to mould you, it feels doubly good. At these times it has relaxed tension in me. It has permitted me to bring out the frightening feelings, the guilt, the despair, the confusion that have been part of my experience. When I have been listened to and when *I have been heard,* I am able to re-perceive my world in a new way and to go on. I have deeply appreciated the times that I have experienced this sensitive emphatic, concentrated listening."[2]

Failure of comprehension or failure to focus attention on what another person is saying, or difficulty in understanding his or her words leads to great dissatisfaction. We may have only heard what we decided the other person is saying. We may twist the message so that the other person says what we want them to say. If we slightly twist a person's words, if we distort the message a little we can make it appear that the other person is not only saying the things we want to hear, but by doing so is the person we want him or her to be. We should know how frustrating it is to be received for what we are not, to be heard to be saying something which we have not said. This creates anger, bafflement and disillusionment.

A large proportion of the New Testament records what Christ said — it also records Him as listening to what other people had to say. He also discussed with His disciples the implications of listening and not listening. The people of Christ's day had: *"grown gross at heart; their ears are dull, and their eyes are closed".* Christ in His explanation of the parable of the sower emphasized that each seed which failed stood for someone who had not **listened** properly, and therefore did not "grow".

A great deal of our failure to communicate stems from the fact that we do not listen properly. It is frustrating when we risk sharing something that is very personal with another individual, and that person receives but does not understand. Creative, sensitive, accurate, non-judgemental listening is vitally important in a meaningful relationship. Growth takes place within us when we can offer this kind of listening to another and also when we have been the recipients of this kind of listening.

Our confidence in prayer is that we have a God who really listens despite all our foolishness and pettiness when we pray. Prayer is not standing on a clifftop and listening to the echo of our voice coming back from the other side of the valley, nor is it like dropping a stone down a deep well or void and hearing the sound. Prayer has been vulgarised as "The Royal Telephone" or as "talking to the Man Upstairs". But believers know that Christian prayer, spoken or unspoken, goes to one place — to God. We do not understand how this miracle happens but we know that from prayer springs up the Christian's *raison d'etre* — if I am in communication with God I know when I have His blessing, when I have His chastisement, and when I have His assurance of love.

3. Clarity of expression

Communication is often hindered because some have difficulty in translating their thoughts into the words which express what they really mean, or feel. It is often assumed the other person has understood what they meant or that they are telepathic and can read the mind of the one trying to communicate! We must strive to present our thoughts clearly.

4. Anger

Many people find conflict unbearable. They would rather smooth over a situation than let feelings of hostility or anger be displayed. This inability to deal with anger frequently results in a breakdown in communication. Feelings of resentment and hostility are repressed and may only surface when triggered off by perhaps some totally irrelevant incident.

We use anger to protect ourselves. We are virtually saying: "I know you are right but I am not going to admit it. So I will attack you instead." This is the basis of all those situation-comedy, married couple arguments.

We fear anger in other people because we interpret it as displeasure and even lack of love. We must separate righteous indignation from petty spite, or annoyance because something has inconvenienced us. Paul wrote to the Ephesians:

> "Throw off falsehood; speak the truth to each other, for all of us are the parts of one body. If you are angry, do not let anger lead you unto sin; do not let sunset find you still nursing it; leave no loop-hole for the devil.
> Ephesians 4:25-26, NEB.

Sometimes anger can be fruitful. We reveal our innermost feelings, and if we are in a group, the group can channel healing to us. It is extraordinary what the dearest folk, the mildest people have bottled up!

We can be angry too about things that are wrong — in our church, in our community and society. This does not mean being judgmental — our wrath can be constructive. Christ did not wait to argue with the money-changers — he cleaned up the Temple. Paul did not hide his annoyance or anger in his letters when it was necessary. Preachers in the past have so emphasized the righteous anger of God that there has been an over-reaction. Christians are not always meek and mild, butter-won't-melt-in-the-mouth people.

5. Self-disclosure

It is significant that one of the marks of revival is confession by Christians to other believers. There have been excesses — that is one of the failings of human-kind.

> "Everyone has his own proper burden to bear." (5).
> "Help one another to carry these heavy loads, and in this way you will fulfil the law of Christ." (3) Galatians 6, NEB.

This does not mean we have to inflate our sins, our burdens into something greater than they are or were. There is no need to "keep up with the Joneses" in confession, nor indulge in sensation-making.

Self-disclosure in a group is a mutual process. The more I know about you and the more you know about me more effective and efficient our communication will be. We cannot bear each other's burdens if we do not know what they are.

Carl R. Rogers talks about "communicating the 'Real' person". He helps us see the importance of not "playing a part" if we are to effectively communicate. Realness or congruence — what I really am and feel and think. This realness, or genuineness, or congruence — whatever term you wish to give it — is a fundamental basis for the best of communication.

If we can be real in our relationships with another person it is very likely to strike some deep note of response to advance our relationship. It also gives a sense of satisfaction when we dare to communicate the realness in us to others — it makes us feel genuine, spontaneous and alive.

We also need courage to allow the other person to be *real* and separate. This allows for the autonomous development of another individual — we are constantly in danger of attempting to mould others into our own image. It is warming and fulfilling to know someone cares for, accepts, admires or prizes me. It is enriching to care for/love another person when I can let that feeling flow out to that person. We should love a person to appreciate him or her — not in order to control them or to have a carbon copy of ourselves. When we can relate this realness in ourselves to others it is very satisfying and it often helps the other person. This also works in reverse. This is the "I-Thou" relationship, as Martin Buber called it.

Because of having less fear of giving or receiving positive feelings we become more able to **appreciate** individuals. We can let them unfold themselves gradually — like a sunset. A person who is loved appreciatively, not possessively, blooms and develops his own unique self. The person who is not prized or appreciated, not only **feels** diminished, he or she **is** diminished.

In a group which is hostile or unappreciative, the person is not worth anything. We need to ensure that the group is receptive to all the needs of those present — that no barriers exist to destroy trust, congruence, understanding and acceptance. People need to be able to relax in order to be themselves. In this way growth in deep personal relationships will take place. We need to remember that we need—

- — a sensitive ability to hear, which results in a deep satisfaction in being heard
- — an ability to be more real which in turn brings forth more realness from the other
- — a willingness to receive warmth and caring from others and consequently a greater freedom to give love.

These elements make interpersonal communication enriching and enhancing.

How to listen to others

"Man does not need to go to the moon or other solar systems. He does not require bigger and better bombs and missiles. He will not die if he does not get better housing or more vitamins . . . His basic needs are few, and it takes little to acquire them, in spite of the advertisers. He can survive on a small amount of bread and in the meanest shelter.

His real need, his most terrible need, is for someone to listen to him, not as a patient, but as a human being of dignity and worth."

(Taylor Caldwell in *The Listener*)

1. Remember that to really listen to another, **there must be a capacity to hear through many wrappings** — listening beyond the outer layer of the spoken word. When a person **really** hears another it puts him or her in touch with that person. It is through hearing people that we have learned all that we know about individuals, about personality, about interpersonal relationships. Sometimes we hear not only the words but also the thought, the depth of feeling, the personal meaning, even the meaning that is below the conscious intent of the speaker — sometimes we hear the deep cry of human need. We must be willing to listen at all levels. In counselling the cry is often heard, "Thank God, somebody heard me. Someone knows what it is like to be me."

2. **Be aware of the possible barriers to the meaning the speaker is trying to convey** — words, images, anxieties, defences, aspirations, decisions. Often people feel a need

to be fully accepted and not misjudged by the listener and will tend to hide their real need behind all means of speech and illustration. We must be sensitive to this need and give them security and trust where they can confidently disclose their most personal thoughts. Nearly all people have a great fear of being rejected, ridiculed or misunderstood.

3. **Be big enough to:**
— **guard against quick judgment of the speaker.** This seals off a real understanding of the speaker. Do not diagnose, appraise or evaluate the speaker. Let the speaker relax, ease any tension and give him or her the freedom he needs to speak. Don't twist the speaker's words in your mind so that you manipulate what you want him or her to say. This leads to frustration, anger and disillusion.

— **guard against labelling the speaker,** so that you listen only to a type and not to a person.

— **guard against trying to impose** upon the other person **a detailed account of your experience,** as if it alone is authentic.

— **openly and honestly engage in a discussion** of the concerns that arise among us.

4. It has been said that
"within each of us there is a **'spectator listener'** who is aware if the other person(s) is listening to him in depth. When the sensitive spectator is not being heard as a person then the 'spectator listener' within each of us signals us not to fully reveal ourselves. We withhold or water down what we really think and feel, because we know that no one is really listening." (Carl R. Rogers)

When people try to share some feeling aspect of themselves which is private, precious or tentative, and this communication is met by evaluation, by no reassurance, by distortion of their meaning, they can react very strongly, despairingly. At such a time one knows what it is like to be alone.

Therefore, to communicate effectively we need—
— **to listen with openness, honesty, acceptance and interest, without judgment.**

— **to listen with expectancy,** so as to evoke the fullest reality and capacity of the person speaking.
— **listen so as to be involved** in what the person is relating.
— **listen with care and concern,** though such listening is never cheap. It costs the listener something of himself.

Dietrich Bonhoeffer writes:

"Many people are looking for an ear that will listen. They do not find it among most people they meet, not even amongst their close friends. But he who can no longer listen to another has lost contact with life. For life is community and community is relationships and relationships die without communication. One who cannot listen long and patiently will presently be talking beside the point and never be really speaking to others; unfortunately, he will not be conscious of it."[3]

"To listen another's soul into a condition of disclosure and discovery may be almost the greatest service that any human being performs for another."

Aids to increasing listening skills

1. Listener should have a **reason** or purpose for listening.

2. Important for Listener to **suspend judgment initially.**

3. Listener should **resist distractions** — noises, views, people — and focus on the speaker.

4. Listener should **wait before responding** to the speaker— too prompt a response reduces listening effectiveness.

5. Listener should **repeat** verbatim or paraphrase what the speaker says.

6. Listener should make sure his **understanding** of the conversation **is to the speaker's satisfaction.**

7. The Listener should **seek the important themes** of what the speaker says by listening through the words for the real meaning.

8. Listener should **allow time to reflect** upon content and to search for meaning.

9. Listener should be **ready to respond** to the speaker's comments.

Don't just listen to words but the meaning behind the words. Listening is not a passive process — it plays an active role in creation. Hearing is done with the ears, while listening is an intellectual, emotional process that integrates physical, emotional and intellectual aspects in a search for acceptance and understanding.

What hinders listening*

lack of interest
lack of concentration
distraction, e.g. t.v.
boredom
preoccupation
non-acceptance
being talked at
verbosity, repetition
class/culture differences
pain, tiredness
fear of rejection

insincerity
assumptions
lack of time
self-consciousness
emotional involvement
lack of training
noise, movement
disagreement
personal convictions
preconceived ideas

unwillingness to become involved
jargon, unable to understand language
inability to understand poor diction
too much information all at once
language limitation, difficulty in understanding
confusion between verbal and non-verbal signals
dislike, personality clash, prejudice
forming wrong first impressions, condemnation
wanting to dominate conversation
lack of empathy or trust
feeling of being "threatened", insecure
trying to work out your answers while the other is
    talking

*Collation of feedback from participants at Small Group courses and workshops.

What helps listening*

knowledge of subject
encouragement
wilingness to listen
not giving advice
honest feedback
adequate eye contact
sensitivity and manner
rapport
time
desire to learn
enthusiasm
clear diction (voice with
    colour)

empathy
environment
non-judgmental
respect for the individual
affirmation
position, closeness
concentration
patience
need
fear
humility

genuine interest and concern
ability to interpret non-verbal signals
acceptance of different views
recognition of importance of subject matters
awareness of prejudices and biases
acceptance of a person for what they are
discipline of thought (thinking before you speak)
being concise, not wordy
attitude of receiver, expectancy/interest draws out the
    disagreement (other can be motivating force)

Inability to deal with anger frequently results in communication breakdown.

Suppression. We often suppress anger for fear that the other person will respond in the same way. We tend to bottle it up until one day it erupts in an emotional avalanche. Unfortunately the other person reacts angrily to our hurried emotional hostility when it often comes out as an attack. **How to cope with angry feelings**

Expression of emotions is important to building good relationships. People need to express their feelings in such a manner that they affirm, reshape and change themselves and others but we need to learn to express angry feelings constructively rather than destructively.

*Collation of feedback from participants at small group courses and workshops.

Helpful guidelines:

1.   Be aware of your emotions.

2.   Admit your emotions — do not ignore or deny them.

3.   Own your emotions — accept responsibility for what you do.

4.   Investigate your emotions. Do not seek for a means of rebuttal to win an argument.

5.   Report your emotions. "Your attitude is beginning to make me feel rather angry." "The feeling I am getting from this discussion is one of irritation (or anger)."

6.   Integrate your emotions with your intellect and your will. Allow yourself to learn and grow as a person.

Emotions **must** be expressed. They should be identified, observed, reported and integrated — then people can make the necessary adjustments in the light of their own ideas of growth.

Some communication skills
Active listening

Five ways of helping persons to understand each other better:

1. Paraphrasing. One of the ways to improve our communication skills is to work at active listening. By active listening is meant more than simply concentrating on what the other person is saying, although that is part of it. It includes letting the other person know that you have heard what he has said.

Very often in conversation, we assume we know what the other person means by a statement, that is, that we understand what the other person intended by his or her remarks. This may be the case, but often we may be missing an important element in the person's communication to us. It is often useful to check to see if we have heard what he really intended to communicate.

The basic skill involved in active listening is paraphrasing or putting into your own words what the other person seems to be communicating to you. This gives him a way to know whether you have missed his point and further clarification is needed. Paraphrasing is letting the other person know the meaning his words have for you in order to test whether or not you have heard what he intended to communicate to you.

Here are some examples:

Ted: There's nothing in church for me any more. None of it makes any sense.

Jack: Church no longer has any meaning for you.

Ted: I wish it did, but I can't believe in God any more.

Jack: You mean the real problem with church is that God doesn't seem real.

Jane: I can't stand the remarks my father makes about my friends! He thinks they're all irresponsible idiots.

Ann: You're angry with him because he doesn't like the friends you choose.

Jane: It's more that he jumps to all the wrong conclusions without making any effort to understand them.

Ann: You wish he didn't write them off so quickly.

Paraphrasing may respond to two dimensions of a communication: the information or content in the communication, and what the person **feels** about the information or content. Sometimes the feeling level will be the real message and at other times almost no feeling at all will be involved. Effective paraphrasing will seek to pick up what the person is really intending.

Jim: I have had it with that son of mine!

Geoff: You sound pretty angry with him.

To paraphrase is not to make a judgment about the other person, who is the only one who knows what he or she really meant. Paraphrasing is a way of testing your understanding of what the other person meant and is always open to being changed. It may not be in the form of a question, but a question mark is always implied. Paraphrasing does not mean approving or agreeing with what the person says, nor is it seeking to reassure or to probe or to argue. It is simply letting the other person know he or she has been heard.

Obviously, paraphrasing is not your only response in a lively conversation. The examples above may seem one-sided because they don't include any feelings or opinions from the person who is responding as you would expect in a typical conversation, it is often a neglected element. This kind of active listening can greatly facilitate good communication.

There are added benefits from paraphrasing. It lets the other person know you're really interested in what he or she is saying. It shows you want to know what he/she means. If the other person feels you can understand his/her point of view he or she is more likely to want to hear **your** point of view. Paraphrasing can also be useful to the other person in helping him/her to clarify his/her own thoughts or feelings by seeing them more objectively or in a different perspective.

2. Perception check. Responses to make sure you are not making false assumptions. Express your own idea of the other person's statement. You may say "I think this is what you meant . . ." "Is that what you meant?" "I feel that you are disturbed. Did my last statement bother you?" "I believe we are agreed to meet at the Post Office corner at five o'clock. Is that correct?"

3. Behaviour description. Reporting the specific acts of another that have an effect on you. "I saw you closing your eyes for a little bit which makes me feel you are very tired." "I saw you jump which made me think you are startled", "I saw your smile turn into a frown which makes me feel you are displeased with me."

Behaviour description leads easily to perception checks: "I saw your smile change to a frown. I feel badly about that. Are you displeased with me?" "I saw you waver and sit down. Are you feeling ill?"

Or, as above, it may lead to direct questions. "You have doubled up your fists and you looked right past me when you spoke to me. Are you angry with me?"

4. Direct questions: Asking questions without any evaluative judgmental words.

5. Describing your own feelings: "I feel warm about your helping me in this way", "I am sad and lonely", "What you have said makes me afraid". "I am very anxious about your trip tomorrow", "I am very upset with you".

Listening, questioning and **observing** are three major categories of communicating.

These take a number of forms:—

Ambulation — how people carry their bodies, whether they swish, amble or stamp. It tells a great deal about who people are and how they are experiencing their environment.

Touching — we can create anger, interest, trust, tenderness, warmth and a variety of other emotions through touch. People differ however in their willingness to touch and be touched. Some give out non-verbal signals which say that they do not wish to be touched.

Eye contact — People tend to size each other up in terms of trustworthiness through reactions to each other's eye contact. Counsellors understand eye contact is an important way of creating understanding and acceptance.

Posturing — How people position their bodies when seated or standing constitute a set of potential signals that may communicate how one is experiencing his or her environment. A person who folds his or her arms and crosses legs is often said to be on the defensive. It is sometimes observed that a person under severe psychological threat will assume the body position of a foetus.

Mannerisms or Tics — This is another form of non-verbal communication — the involuntary nervous spasms of the body can be a key when one feels threatened. Some people stammer or jerk but these mannerisms can be easily misinterpreted.

Subvocals — sounds uttered when trying to find words, e.g. uh, um, er. We say a lot of non-word things in order to carry a meaning to another person. We hum, grunt, groan, etc. — they are not words, purely noise, but they do carry meaning.

Distancing — each person is said to have a psychological space around him. If someone invades that space he may become tense, alert, etc. We tend to place distance between ourselves and others according to the kinds of relationship that we have and what our motives are toward each other.

Gesturing — Gestures carry a great deal of meaning but gestures do not mean the same things to all people. Gestures give emphasis to our words and often clarify our meanings.

Vocalism — as an example, "I love my children". That sentence is meaningless unless it is pronounced. The way that sentence is packaged vocally determines the signal it gives to another person. Depending where the emphasis is placed determines the meaning another is likely to infer from our message.

References:
1. Cecil Osborne, *The Art of Understanding Yourself* (Zondervan Books, 1972).
2. Carl R. Rogers, *Some Elements of Effective Impersonal Communication*. A transcript of talks given at the California Institute of Technology, Pasadena, California, Nov. 9, 1964.
3. Dietrich Bonhoeffer, *Life Together* (S.C.M. Press, 1963).

Other books consulted:
Philip A. Anderson, *Church Meetings that Matter* (United Church Press, 1965, p. 28, 30.
Sara Little, *Learning Together in the Christian Fellowship* (John Knox Press, 1965).
Lawrence O. Richards, *A New Face for the Church* (Zondervan, 1971).

Other sources:
A number of roneoed resource sheets and short articles from the Yokefellow Institute, Richmond, Indiana, and the Programme Council of the Iowa United Methodist Conference, Des Moines, Iowa. Unfortunately, the authors' names were not indicated.
Material in a number of *Annual Handbooks for Group Facilitators,* by Pfeiffer and Jones (University Associates, California, 1972, 1973, 1974) has also been drawn upon in this chapter.

10   Resolution of Conflict

Graeme Beattie

"Conflict frightens me. I always avoid it whenever I can."

"I don't like it when things get tense. So I try to be pleasant and not upset anyone. I just say what people want to hear."

"It doesn't matter to me what people think. I'll say and do what I please!"

"Conflict? What conflict? We're just having a good discussion!"

I suppose we have all been in situations where we have experienced these attitudes to conflict. Perhaps some of them reflect how we ourselves, deep down, feel about facing conflict. There seem to be four main attitudes or ways in which we cope with conflict. Many are frightened by conflict situations and either try to escape the scene or smooth over the troubled waters without getting to the root of the problem.

Others either refuse to face up to the reality of conflict — "We are just having a good discussion" — or have become so used to protecting their own egos that they totally disregard the feelings and viewpoints of those opposed to them. Our reactions to conflict are both instinctive and learned. We want acceptance, love and security and we want to avoid hurt, pain and rejection, encounter and disagreement. Conflict, suffering and tension are avoided as much as possible.

Jesus made it very clear to any would-be disciple that His Way meant and means that we will encounter suffering and will encounter conflict.

"You must not think that I have come to bring peace to the earth; I have not come to bring peace, but a sword. I have come to set a man against his father, a daughter against her mother, a young wife against her mother-in-law; and a man will find his enemies under his own roof."

(*Matthew* 10, 34-36, *NEB*)

Jesus lived a life of authentic person to person encounter in which He creatively confronted and used human conflict. He did not avoid conflict with the pharisees and the religious authorities.

Conflict and tension can never be avoided by the Christian. It is part and parcel of our call to discipleship. It is interesting too that the behavioural scientists affirm that conflict and tension are vital for human growth and maturity. Unfortunately we tend to think of conflict as always being something negative. We are inclined to respond to conflict in a programmed, computer-like manner. Our read-out probably goes something like this:

CONFLICT

BAD

ISOLATE IT BY:

    (1) Ignoring it

    (2) Eliminating it

    (3) Subjugating it

    (4) Compromising with it

    (5) Developing alliances against it

IMPORTANT FACTOR: ELIMINATE CONFLICT AS SOON AS POSSIBLE.

Sounds familiar? Even though you may not be consciously aware of it that is the way most of us automatically react to conflict — just like a computer, having been programmed that way from early childhood.

But the truth is that not all conflict is "bad". Actually there are three levels of conflict:—

Minus	Neutral	Plus
violence	competition	drama
war	bargaining	fun
death	mediation	adventure
destruction	scarcity	opportunity
disorder	reconciliation	excitement
aggression	tension	development

Although the minus factors are undesirables, the person who is ready to creatively cope with conflict can turn even these into learning experiences that will be advantageous. For example, a death in a family can become a creative opportunity to face up to and accept our own humanity and the healing support of God's grace.

Robert Dow succintly expresses the value of conflict when he writes:

> "The very word 'conflict' implies 'to fight together'. To have a conflict, there must be, by mutual agreement, an encounter. Any encounter can lead to resolve, reconciliation and growth. (Growth here implies new learning and new behaviour.) In trust we take the risk that conflict may not lead to good results. High trust — high risk — high productivity. At times, high trust and high risk mean a cross. This is the risk of the actualized person."[1]

As we can see from the above quotation, conflict faced rationally and creatively leads to personal growth and new learning. Conflict encountered in trust frees us to lead a vibrant and fulfilled life, for no growth, no real learning that will lead to a change in behaviour, can take place without conflict.

> "Consider now all the creative factors you have experienced in your life. Do they really come in times of quiet and inactivity? Or have they not come, sometimes by accident, in the midst of, or just after, some struggle? Conflict can be an agent of growth."[2]

145

Conflict develops out of raw human interaction. It is when we interact sensitively but honestly with one another in our groups and in life in general, that we ourselves begin to change, to grow, to blossom. There is a certain tough-mindedness about the Christian way of life that calls us to "speak the truth in love" and to be free to be angry with each other without allowing the anger to become unclean by festering into bitterness and resentment (cf. Ephesians 4: 15 & 25-26). Conflict that is avoided or suppressed will turn sour and pollute the life of our groups with destructive results. The love that Jesus calls us into is a caring toughness that acknowledges "God did not give us a spirit of timidity but a spirit of power and love and self-control" (2 Timothy 1:7). In that creative spirit we are freed to face conflict and tension and so blossom as children of God.

How do we go about successfully managing conflict in our group life? We each have our own way of approaching conflict situations and even when these approaches are unsuccessful, we often continue to use them because we know no other alternatives. **Responding to conflict**

We can classify our strategy for handling conflict into three categories: avoidance, defusion and confrontation. We have already stated that avoiding the conflict is no answer. Ignoring the "stirrer" in a group or pretending that people "don't really mean what they say" in the heat of an argument helps no one and gets nowhere. While it's a good idea to avoid a charging bull, you can't get away from unresolved conflict in an ongoing group. If that conflict is not squarely faced and properly handled it will simmer below the surface and pollute the relationships within the group.

Some people think that conflict is like a bomb. If you can't avoid it then defuse it! But defusion is a delaying tactic. You may try to cool off the situation by aiming to resolve minor points while avoiding or delaying discussion on the major problem. Invariably defusion results in feelings of dissatisfaction and frustration towards the leader, "problem" person or the group as a whole, and anxiety about the future and one's own image.

The third way of responding to conflict is by an actual

confrontation between the conflicting issues or people. But confrontation itself can be further subdivided into **power** strategies and **negotiation** strategies. Power strategies mean the use of physical force (e.g. a punch in the nose); bribery (e.g. gifts, favours); and punishment (e.g. witholding love, money) to settle the conflict. From the point of view of the "winner" such tactics are often quite effective. Unfortunately, hostility, anxiety, resentment and physical retaliation are generally the "loser's" reaction to these win-lose power tactics. And such reactions are totally destructive not only regarding the relationship between "winner" and "loser" but for the entire group. As a group consists of a system of interdependent relationships of people pursuing some common purpose or goal, nothing can happen to one member in the group without the whole group life being affected.

On the other hand, with negotiation strategies both sides can win. The aim of negotiation is to resolve the conflict with a compromise or a solution which all the parties involved would find acceptable and satisfying. Therefore negotiation is regarded as the most positive conflict management strategy.

The conflict management process

Successful conflict management requires the knowledge and practice of necessary negotiation skills.

(1) Diagnosis of the nature of the conflict

In this first step the important thing is to determine whether the conflict is a "value" conflict (i.e. one arising out of different life attitudes and values) or a "real" (tangible) conflict, or a combination of both. "Value" conflicts are very difficult to resolve. For example, if, as a member of a group discussing the place of children in church worship services, you firmly believed that children could not meaningfully participate, while I felt that all ages could significantly worship together, it could be quite difficult for us to arrive at a mutually agreeable position.

However, a difference in values is only really significant when our opposing views affect us in some real or tangible way. Continuing the above example, if that discussion group were changed into a task group to plan a morning worship service, our differing views regarding children in church now present us with a negotiable conflict. It is not necessary

147

for either of us to change our values in order for us and the whole task group to come to a mutually agreeable position. For example, we may design the worship service as a family service using a liturgy that has something to say to all age groups.

So it is important to determine whether the conflict is a "real" or a "value" conflict. If it is a conflict in differing personal values that in no way affects the life of the group, then we should respect one another's rights to differ, and leave it at that. However, most conflict situations in small groups are "real" conflicts that do affect the life of the group and its different members, and as such need to be resolved.

(2) Effectiveness in initiating and confronting a conflict

Having determined that the conflict is a "real" conflict, it is then necessary to be able to skilfully confront the conflict. Here it is important not to begin by attacking or belittling the opposing party. A defensive reaction on either side will block any effective resolution. The most effective way to approach the situation is to state the actual effects the conflict has on you personally, or on the group. If the conflict directly affects the whole group, invite other members to check out how they are affected. For example, you are in a church youth group planning an evening outing. One member suggests a night right in the middle of your examination timetable. Other members of your group are doing exams too. Your best approach would be something like, "Well, I have a problem with that night. I've got a heavy exam the next morning. How does it suit others?" This would be much more effective than saying, "That's just like you. Just because you're not studying, you don't have any consideration for those who have exams!"

(3) Hearing the other's point of view

Perhaps your initial statement (as in 2 above) will not meet with a sympathetic response from your opponent. Then it becomes vital to listen to and really hear what the other party is saying. He or she may react with a defensive counter argument or a hard-line approach. Avoid making argument-provoking replies. Don't try to defend yourself, don't explain your position, and don't make threats, or demands. Instead listen to, and reflect back to the other person, in your own words, what he or she is saying. For example, our friend in (2) above might reply to your "problem" with, "Ah, you students are all the same, always worried about exams. You'll get through. Besides I've got to work that next day, and every day, not just when exams are on."

It would be easy here to jump in and defend yourself. But hold on — play it cool. Listen to what the other person is saying and reflect it back. "I hear you saying that you think I'm being over-anxious about my exams and that I'm not really sensitive to the problems and pressures that you people who have a job to go to every day, have to face. Is that right?" Showing that you have listened to your opponents and checking out their position will lower their defences. You have indicated that you have made an effort to begin to understand their viewpoint. As a result they will be more ready to hear your point of view. So only then should you present your position, being careful to avoid value statements (such as "No one really understands the pressures students face at exam time."), and concentrating on outcomes that are tangible and not abstract ideas and values. In this way, not only is the road opened for a resolution of the immediate conflict but you are starting to build a bridge of understanding between yourself and the other person that will lead to improved relationships and greater honesty within the group.

(4) Problem solving

The final skill needed to resolve a conflict is the use of the problem solving process by the group to reach a decision that is agreeable to all. The steps in problem solving are:—

i) **Clarify the problem** — The above skills in diagnosing the nature of the conflict, initiating a confrontation, and listening to the other's point of view are important here. The group should consider: what is the real issue or concern here that effects us; what is its cause; and how does each of us stand concerning this issue?

ii) **Establish objectives** — What is the purpose of the decision you wish to reach? What are your specific objectives regarding that decision?

149

iii) **Generate alternative solutions** — Brainstorm as many alternative solutions as you can. Don't worry about how wild or way out they may seem. They'll be evaluated later.

iv) **Evaluate alternatives against objectives** — Okay, now evaluate those "wild" alternatives against the purpose and objectives of your desired decision.

v) **Assess alternatives against adverse consequences** — From step (iv), what two or three alternatives best seem suited? What possible disadvantages does any have? What could go wrong with any one of them?

vi) **Select best alternative** — Remember that this is to be a group decision. You are to decide together (**not** voting) on the best solution. The one solution most acceptable to all (in the light of the above steps) should be chosen.

vii) **Plan to implement the solution** — How, when, and where will the solution be carried out? What preventative steps can be taken in case something should go wrong?

viii) **Implement the solution** — Okay, now put the solution into practice.

ix) **Evaluate the solution** — In spite of all the above steps the solution you chose may not have been the best or most workable. So plan to evaluate your solution after a specified period of time. If your solution does prove to have flaws, the problem solving process should begin again from step (i).

A final word for group leaders

It goes without saying that the role of the group leader in conflict management is especially important. In addition to acquiring the above skills the leader should be aware that in the initial stages of a conflict, the group members must feel that the leader is strong, competent and personally secure enough to be able to stand in the middle of an aggressive confrontation. Furthermore, the climate in the group needs to be an open one with evident trust, if a resolution is to be reached. Members must be encouraged to accept their own feelings, hold their own values, and strengthen those ideas which seem to be most helpful to them. Also, try and limit the number of conflicts being handled at once. Generally people find they can handle one or two disconcerting things but not a large number at the same time.

In conflict management there is a tendency for people to "get honest". The leader should be aware of those members who tend to use "honesty" as a whip and/or a hiding place. There is a real difference between being "honest" and "truthful". In a confrontation it is possible for a person to be honest in his rage, but this hostility can easily be a defence rather than legitimate anger. "His rage may still be toward someone who is taking the brunt of things for the "father" he never had, rather than toward a person in the here and now. This transference needs to be carefully worked through. Verbalization will often allow this filtering, as it does in a more positive transference experience".[3]

Finally, although He did not seek it out, Jesus was a man who faced conflict well and used it, regardless of from where or from whom it came. He refused to "play it safe". As Robert Dow suggests, can we who follow Him do less?

References:

1. Robert Arthur Dow, *Learning Through Encounter* (Judson Press, 1971), p. 149.
2. ibid, p. 154.
3. ibid, page 157.

11 How to Commence Small Groups

There is no magical formula, no set pattern to follow when commencing a small group. The history of small groups in the church shows that they commence in a variety of ways. It is helpful to know how other groups commenced. Some guidelines will emerge if we study how people have been drawn togther. We need, however, to ensure and preserve flexibility, for the way your group commences may have some similarity or it may be entirely different.

How some groups began

In the chapter "Types of Small Groups" we have given some feed-back received during basic small groups conferences when participants were asked to list the types of small group experiences in which they had been involved. Later in the conference, when we look at how to commence small groups, they were asked to share on the basis of these questions — How did a small group with which you have been previously associated commence? What was the initial motivation? The following is a collection of the answers which were given.

- I was not achieving and felt I wanted fellowship with others to help me grow.
- There was a lack of depth in the fellowship available in my church.
- After a house-party experience I felt a deep desire to extend the depth of fellowship and learning which took place over that weekend.
- A number of us were in like circumstances in a college and expressed the desire for support.
- I wanted to improve a skill.
- We had been given a common task to fulfil.
- It was a tradition in our church to work through small groups. They had been successful in helping people grow so I wanted to join one.

- I had a need for self acceptance which I felt could be met in a group.
- I was lonely and insecure.
- A number of us felt we wanted a continuing situation in which we could be encouraged, supported, affirmed and loved.
- I felt I needed the stimulation from others to be consistent.
- I had a deep desire to share with others where I really was at spiritually. I wanted to be honest. I wanted to learn more.
- A desire to develop meaningful relationships with others.
- We wanted to break down the barriers which exist between age groups.
- A number of us wanted to show concern for others outside the church *(Repeated)*.
- My problem was communication with others — this led me to seek out a group.
- In fellowship with others I felt I could achieve a goal which was not possible on my own.
- Someone invited me to join the group to which they belonged.
- A group which had grown too large divided.
- I liked the informality of a group in contrast to the formal fellowship in rigid worship services.
- One person was the driving force *(Repeated)*.
- It was commenced as a follow-up to an outreach programme.
- As a couple we wanted to meet with other couples who were experiencing similar problems.

In the main these groups commenced because: (i) There was a common interest. (ii) There was a deep sense of need. (iii) One person had initiative and vision.

These generalizations are supported from further feed-in at these conferences after groups had read sections of *Taste of New Wine* and *Second Touch* by Keith Miller, *Miracle on the River Kwai* by Ernest Gordon, and *With the Holy Spirit and with Fire* by Samuel Shoemaker. After seeking to learn from each writer about how small groups commence the groups reported:

- The initiator shared honestly and openly a deep sense of need with others.
- The group began in an informal manner.

— One person took the initiative to seek out others who felt the same way.

— There was a common feeling for something better.

— The witness of others helped motivate the need.

— There was a willingness to give it a go.

— They all needed each other.

— There was a convergence of events which drew the group together.

— One insignificant person gave himself wholly to God.

— It doesn't take a saint to start a group!!!

— People can't be coerced into joining a group.

— Often the least likely person will want to join.

— The Holy Spirit was the key factor.

— Having found others with a common need they didn't procrastinate — a definite time and place was set.

— The leader didn't have all the answers but he was prepared to search for them.

— The Holy Spirit directed but He needed individuals who were responsive and available but not necessarily with great ability.

— There was a hunger for knowledge and a gripping sense of need for purpose and meaning in their lives.

— A willingness to be open to real risk in sharing their own real lives.

— Started as a call — not as a gimmick.

— Need to share a vision in order not to lose it.

From these observations we can deduce that:

The common interest and sense of need as a necessary pre-requisite are further supported.

The significant role played by an inadequate person who was nevertheless open and available is established.

The need to make definite plans to get together once a number feel drawn together is imperative if the initial vision and motivation is not to be lost in vagueness and indecision.

The prime role of the Holy Spirit in awakening the sense of need, giving a vision of how this need can be met and enabling the initiator and participants, is a deep insight which should always be kept in mind.

John L. Casteel sums up these findings: "Groups come into being when the hunger, faith and determination of concerned persons are matched with the leading and empowerment of the Holy Spirit."[1]

Gaining a vision of what it is like to belong to a caring, concerned, redeeming small community of people is a very necessary first step if small groups are to be vital. "Unless there be a consciousness of the significance of groups and their possibilities, leaders are not likely to improve those now existing or to set up new ones to fill new purposes."[2] Potential members will also need to be helped gain such a vision of the role the small group experience can be expected to play in meeting their needs and those of others. **Helping others see the potential**

Reports of others who have been in groups can be valuable in helping people see the potential of the small group. A living witness always helps motivate the sceptic who needs "proof". A small group of lay people whose lives have been touched by this process can be a strong encouragement to others. At Port Kembla and Liverpool Methodist Churches, individual members would often be asked to share their experience of the value of the small group with church members in other areas. I made cassette recordings of some testimonies which I take with me when called in to consult with parishes about this means of renewal. Whenever we conducted a lay witness week-end most of the team would be members of our small groups and inevitably spontaneous sharing about the value of the small group experience would take place during the supper groups. Some parishes have invited a team to conduct a conference or series of special meetings to help the parish see the possibilities of small groups in bringing renewal. These conferences are headed up by a minister who has successful small groups in his own parish. A team of lay people involved in these groups share the leadership and bring rich first-hand experiences to bear. They also are available for consultation and witness apart from the conference. The overflow of lives enriched by small groups are a powerful means of helping others catch the vision.

Written accounts of the experiences of people will be helpful. These appear in Christian magazines from time to time or in roneoed reports of significant small group work. There are many books on the market today linked with the small group movement. Some, like Keith Miller's and Bruce

Larson's, tell of the search for spiritual renewal which found fulfilment in a small group experience. Others treat the subject directly and show how new life came into local parishes through small groups. Books by Elizabeth O'Connor, Michael Skinner, Robert Girard, Robert Raines, Lawrence Richards and others are helpful and are recommended to hand to thoughtful people. I made it a policy in parish work to keep books circulating amongst my people which had helped me catch a new vision for various facets of our ministry. Then it wasn't a superimposed programme from on top but a moving forward together.

There are a number of pre-recorded cassettes which you could lend to people on the value of small groups by people involved in vital small groups. Recorded lectures by leaders in the small group movement are also available. Creative Resources (Word Inc.) have titles by Bruce Larson, Gordon Cosby, Keith Miller and Lyman Coleman. There are also a number of cassettes of feed-in to our conferences by a number of people available from the N.S.W. Board of Education of the Uniting Church.

A variety of methods can be used to help people discover for themselves the value of small groups. There are a number of worksheets available which are useful for this task, or they can be designed to meet the local situation without requiring special skills. On page 12 of his book *69 Ways to Start a Study Group and Keep it Growing,* Lawrence D. Richards lists some dimensions of relationship of which the Bible speaks. Next to each he provides a graded check line to help individuals check out their own life and decide if perhaps they need to become involved in a group. This could be varied in a number of ways to cover the characteristics of a Christian community or aspects of a Christian style of life which are developed in relation to others, etc. Against these lists people could measure their individual and collective Christian life. It could help awaken a sense of need for the growth which is possible in a small group.

On two occasions in my parish work the local membership caught the vision during a Church Life Conference. We considered the New Testament pattern and characteristics of church life. Against this model we evaluated our existing life within the local community of faith. Alternative styles were considered. Out of this reflection by the members grew significant small group work amongst youth and adults. In both cases I circulated a variety of books for thoughtful individuals to read in the three and four months prior to each conference.

Other ways of leading people to see the potential of small groups were given by participants in our training conferences in brain-storming sessions. There are some suggestions worth thinking about.

- Use the individual approach.
- Share your own sense of need for a group.
- Use the small group method in as many aspects of your leadership as possible until people see their value, e.g. in teaching, planninig, evaluating and in meetings of larger groups.
- Learn to depend on the Holy Spirit to lead you to people who have the same need, then share how the small group can help.
- Personal enthusiasm.
- Listen to people.
- Have an open home to which people will feel free to come and informally experience care in a small group.
- Share resources and experiences gained at a Small Groups Conference with others.
- Invite others to accompany you to Small Group Training Conferences.
- Use small groups in church services — even just getting people to discuss or share in pairs.
- Pray until you are convinced about sharing your need with a person.
- Talk about small groups — how others have been helped — what they have meant to you.
- Demonstrate the value of small groups through your own growth.
- Provide opportunities for people to think about the best methods for the church to fulfil its work and witness. Introduce them to small groups as a viable method.

Two ways to begin

Start small and let it grow. Probably most groups have been started because just one or two people really felt the need for them.

Two or three motivated persons who have a desire to grow in fellowship and faith are enough to begin a group.

It is better to begin to develop a group with a small number of well-intentioned persons who can encounter one another at some depth because of their sense of need for such an experience, than to begin with a large number who come with reservations. From a small but sound beginning the group can pray that God will either send to them or send them to people who should be in their group. Lyman Coleman, in his prologue to *Growth by Groups,* says, "One man with a genuine hunger is enough to start a group. One group is enough to penetrate a community. The question is not one of quantity, but quality."[3]

One small group to which I belong began by just two of us sharing our need for fellowship and opportunity to share and support each other in our similar leadership roles. We decided to meet infrequently for lunch together then later became aware of others who had similar needs. A breakfast group eventuated involving five others. I have met with one other person for a number of years to share and pray together. Both of us find this a viable group through which we have been able to enter into deep levels of openness and experienced support and encouragement through a number of crisis situations. We have been open to inviting others to join with us but have never felt guided to any particular persons. It seems this experience is intended to play a unique part in our Christian lives to supplement the other small groups to which we belong.

Start big and let it shake down: Some will be guided to gather a large number of people together for a one time meeting at which the concept of small groups will be presented. From this a number of small groups may eventuate. If considerable interest has been aroused in a church by a special programme of outreach or renewal it would be wise to capitalise on this new enthusiasm and call a special gathering of people to talk over the possibility of organising some groups. This interest has frequently been generated after a Lay Witness Weekend and alert local leaders have 'struck while the iron was hot'. A number of small groups have eventuated, to nurture new Christians.

Both of our small groups programmes for adults in Port Kembla Uniting Church and Hamilton Wesley Church began with a Saturday evening dinner attended by close to 200 in each case. At Hamilton the initial interest grew out of a Church Life Conference. At Port Kembla the thrust came because of the new life resulting from a Billy Graham evangelistic campaign. Those who made commitments were given weekly training for six months and surrounded with a complex personal support system before 46 were received into membership of the church. These people later became the nucleus for 12 groups involving 140 people.

On occasions a large group of 20 or more have met for a period in a seminar type meeting to give teaching in Christian beliefs which has provided a foundation for a later small groups programme. Work in small groups has taken place in the large meeting helping participants become used to the process. This larger meeting has then divided to form the nucleus of a number of house centred cells.

Initial motivation of a core group. We have already seen that there will be little or no motivation to link up with a small group where there is not a sense of need. The awakening of this awareness of need, I have found, generally comes at an unexpected time. If it is truly of God, and not a fruit of man's manipulation, it appears to be seldom planned. There have been times when my church leaders and I have planned and prayed for an event which we hoped would bring renewal but it resulted in only a very small discernible response. However, this does not mean we should make no plans and cease to pray for new life in the church. It is imperative however that we be sensitive to the working of the Spirit and the inner stirrings which people express often in a veiled manner. Motivation for spiritual growth is essentially the work of the Spirit.

At Port Kembla the initial motivation was an evangelistic mission, at Hamilton and Liverpool, a Church Life Conference. With others it has been a renewal retreat, a Lay Witness Week-end or other forms of outreach, and with others various forms of Conferences. Without this motivation by at least a small core group to seek after new and deeper spiritual growth generally an abortive programme results.

Seek to develop a wider interest. This can be done by using the media available to us in a local parish. At Hamilton in the period between the leaders catching the vision at a Church Life Conference and the planned commencement of the small group programme I preached a series of sermons on the early church, looking at the quality of its life and witness. Other sermons focused on the ministry of Jesus, his calling of the 12 and their life together. A series of biographical sermons traced individual encounters with Jesus, the renewal which took place and the nurture provided.

Commencing a cluster of small groups

In *New Life in the Church*, Robert Raines published the sermons which preceded the formation of his significant small group in one parish. They are worth perusing to gather ideas for helping to provide this development of interest. Articles in the parish paper giving the rationale for small groups, reports of successful groups and testimonies of individuals who have been enriched through such experiences all heighten interest. A number of suitable films and filmstrips are available which could be used at appropriate times. The section in this chapter on "Helping Others see the Potential of Small Groups" gives further ideas.

Enlist and train potential leaders. At Port Kembla this happened before we caught the vision of the possibilities of small groups! I never cease to be amazed at the way God works out His purposes frequently without us being aware of it at the time. Often it is only in retrospect we see the plan. As I have already pointed out we gathered together the people referred to the Church from the Billy Graham Crusade to establish them in their new-found faith and prepare them for membership. Others joined with them and over 70 people packed into the parsonage lounge room each week for these sessions! The evening included informal fellowship, praise, group prayer, an illustrated lecture and discussion. After two years the number dwindled to twenty-five. We sought to discern what God was saying to us through this decline in interest. Through a series of events. while absent from the church, I caught the vision of the potential of small groups. This was shared with the remaining twenty-five and we decided to make the group a training ground for potential leaders (and co-leaders). We struggled to learn something about how small groups function, develop some leadership skills and evolve a plan to introduce our vision to the congregations.

These leaders received a preparation for their tasks which few small group leaders experience. Crash programmes don't include the teaching in doctrine, introduction to the Bible and Church History which these leaders experienced for nearly two years, together with the significant group experience. Too often we are content with a crash course in small group techniques without the development in knowledge and understanding of the Christian faith. It is little wonder so many small groups are superficial and deteriorate into a sharing of ignorance.

Enlist potential members. This seems a heavily structured manner to enlist people without some of the freedom and spontaneity I have been advocating. However, past experience has proved this to be an authentic way to begin in certain situations. There is no set way to commence small groups. A list of prospects can be compiled by the potential leaders going through the lists of those associated with church. This has a distinct drawback as often the least likely person will want to be involved. At Liverpool we commenced the youth cells and the adult cells in this way. A similar method was used at Port Kembla. The names extracted from the church lists were divided into geographical areas and a leader assigned to each section. Most leaders received a list of up to 30 names but ended up with an average of 12 in their final group. The leaders visited each person on their list drawing attention to the prior publicity in the church paper and special mailings. They gave further information and invited them to attend a launching dinner as a sample small group experience. A blanket invitation was given to the whole church by mail and pulpit announcements to ensure that no one felt left out or overlooked.

At Hamilton the whole church was invited to a launching dinner at which the new programme was outlined. Response forms were issued upon which people indicated their interest and the nights they were available. Further forms were available at the weekly church services for those not able to attend the dinner. These were then sorted into common times and geographical areas. The leaders assigned then visited each person in their group and invited them to an inaugural meeting in the host home.

When commencing the 10 youth cells at Liverpool which involved 120 young people we began by making a comprehensive list. This comprised all young people in the existing youth groups and others from past and present Sunday school rolls. These we then divided into groups based upon age, locality and mutual interest. Most groups contained a balance of "actives" and "inactives". By "inactives" is meant young people who have little or no association with the church. Difficulty was later experienced in some groups where there was a greater number of inactives. Less groups with a better balance would have made the task more effective. Greater depth would have resulted thus preparing the groups for future outreach to their own peer group.

The counsellors appointed visited the home of each young person assigned to them which permitted a discussion with the parents about the new programme and established an important personal contact.

In the setting up of one small group programme in a Presbyterian parish, where I was called in to act as consultant, we used the elder's districts as the basis for the groups. Each elder was trained as a group leader and visited those in his district to invite them to join a group in most cases held in the elder's home. In two or three districts where there was little response the elders combined their groups and acted as co-leaders.

Robert Raines and others have taken a long term approach when commencing clusters of small groups. Their method, in brief, was to lead a cell themselves until the group became established (the time this takes varied from group to group). As experienced group facilitators they modelled a good leadership style. The group learned about leadership and small group techniques by demonstration. The leader recognized and developed potential leadership within the group, until he felt confident he could relinquish his leadership. He then commenced another group, repeating the process. There is much to be said for the long-term approach.

Commencing a single cell

As we have observed previously, there is no one way to commence a small group. Each group is unique. No two small group experiences are exactly the same. We consider here some possible alternatives for commencing a single cell.

Check your motives. The Faith at Work small group movement recommends that we begin with a period of self-examination in which we ask ourselves two questions: "Why do I want to start a small group?" and "Why do I need a small group?". The suggestion that answers be written down and considered will help us in clarifying our motives and the expectations we have from such a group. This will assist us in our approach to others. We will be better able to express our hopes and aspirations for the group when talking to others. The type of group which will best meet these needs will be clearer.

Listen for expressed needs which can be met in small groups.

In taking the initiative we need to do so with sensitivity to people who are aching for this type of experience. Often they are not communicating it verbally, at least in direct terms. I shall never forget the advice Professor Ross Snyder of Chicago gave to a number of us in this regard. He led

163

us in a variety of small group experiences over a number of days and thoroughly whetted our appetites for an ongoing group experience when we returned home again. At the conclusion he advised us not to rush into drawing a group together. "Take time to really listen to people. Seek to recognize their inner stirrings. Listen between the words they use, for veiled expressions of a deep heart-felt need which can be met in a small group. Some will be crying out to you from the depth of their inner being 'I want to belong. I long to be wanted. I desperately want to grow', without so much as using any of these words". When I returned home I put this advice into practise and it worked! My first experience of sharing openly and honestly in a small group was an unforgettable freeing and renewing experience. That group which meant so much to me in a period of trauma and searching came together because of this method of seeking to be sensitive to expressed needs. It was made up of the most unlikely people drawn from a broad cross-section of the community. Not in my wildest dreams would I have imagined that such a group would have emerged to help me on a long road to credibility.

Listening is an art which requires time and practice. Hearing people express the desire to belong to a group will occur when least we expect it. We will be best tuned in to people when we are tuned in to God. Sensitivity to spiritual need is a gift of divine grace. When I fail to live at the centre I must miss many distress signals from those I meet in everyday contacts.

Take the initiative yourself. Sometimes God will guide us to be more direct in approaching others. That sounds as if I am contradicting what I said in the last section. I'm sorry! But the Spirit refuses to restrict His mode of operation. Experience shows He has no set pattern. In some situations it will be right for us to not wait for others to make the first move. Be the first member yourself! A test of our own readiness to become an active participant in a small group lies in our willingness to make the effort to do all we can to encourage the formation of a group. At the same time we will make ourselves available to God for him to direct in the way which coincides with His plan and purpose.

Test interest by giving a book to a selected group of people. Pray about who could be invited to link up with a group. Select a book which fits in with the expectations you have for the group. If you have a deep need to mature in your spiritual experience choose contemporary books on spiritual growth by authors such as Keith Miller, Bruce Larson, Katherine Marshall, Rosalind Rinker, Eugenia Price (for women), Cecil Osborne, Karl Olsson and others. Buy a few paperback copies and distribute to those you feel drawn to. Some may have already communicated an interest in linking up with a small group. Say you would like them to read it and meet together in a few weeks to share their reaction. Don't mention you are hoping to start a continuing group. This method tests people's sense of need. Give a precise period for reading and set a date for a supper or daytime get-together. Keep the meeting informal and let the Spirit move in the way He wishes. Each should be given opportunity to share their thoughts and feelings about the book. Openly receive both negative and positive responses.

At the conclusion of the group some may spontaneously express the desire to meet again to discuss the same book more fully, possibly taking a chapter at a time over a number of meetings. The wish may be to take another book and deal with it in the same way. Don't expect everyone to continue with the group. It may not be their thing — so don't coerce. From such an experience a small group could begin. It tests interest without specific commitment to a continuing group and the one-time meeting can be of value in itself even if it doesn't result in the formation of a group.

Provide "sample" small group experiences. People can be given a one-time small group experience to help them see the potential of belonging to a small group. This is similar to the previous point but without the requirement for preparation prior to the group. The chapter on "Outreach and Nurture" and "At Homes" gives some suggestions for this type of experience. Once again, the group should be kept informal. Some Relationship Games such as those found in the companion volume to this book *(Creative Ideas for Groups)* which provide a completely non-threatening experience could be used. At the conclusion, a test of their readiness to go on into a continuing group could be made by simply asking "Would you like to meet again to undertake some similar activities?" A series of these low key groups may be needed before the group decides to be an on-going group and formulate goals and guidelines for its continuance.

Use a Camp or Retreat Situation.

Most church camps or retreats provide a variety of

small group experiences which introduce people to the quality of fellowship possible in the small group. Some retreats I have led have placed people in a small group for the entire period. Study, worship, recreation, kitchen duties and the like, have all been undertaken in the small group, with only occasional combined activity. This is an adaptation of the T-Group or Encounter Group and would need to be explained and agreed upon by the participants prior to the retreat.

Generally such a retreat would be only for those who express a willingness to participate in a small group for a definite length of time. It is important that such retreats take people out of their familiar surroundings and give them uninterrupted involvement.

Treat Early Group Experiences as Experimental. Most of us hesitate to commit ourselves to new experiences and programmes that don't have a clear cut-off point. For this reason, suggest a specific number of meetings in a set period of times when once the group decides to be ongoing. Six to eight meetings on a weekly or bi-weekly basis is a reasonable period. This gives the experience an experimental quality and encourages a definite commitment. At the end of the time the experience can be assessed and a decision made whether or not to continue.

Pray About It. The setting up of small groups in the name of Jesus Christ is essentially God's work. Our task is basically that of co-operating with what God is already doing in His world. In prayer, we acknowledge this, make ourselves available to God, check on our motives, develop the right attitude and seek to make God's timing our timing. As we pray, God can strengthen our desire and resolve to start a group, or He can make it clear that we should wait for some other opportunity.

One of the "midwives" of Holy Spirit who helped bring to life the quite new small group revolution in the U.S.A. was the late episcopal bishop, Sam Shoemaker. He gives us some words of wisdom in *With the Holy Spirit and with Fire,* to conclude this chapter.

'People sometimes say or write me "How do you organize one of these small groups?" and the answer is, you can't organize them, any more than you can organize a love affair or a great poem. Groups are organic, i.e., they come about through the impact of life upon life. You can bring together a dozen spiritual-minded people, and nothing of any significance may happen at all.

'One never knows where the Holy Spirit may come into a relationship or a company and give it His own stamp of meaning and power. Perhaps the first question is not whether we want to start a group, but whether He does? If He does, He must ordinarily find someone who is open to such direction and leadership. It does not take great saints, else none of us would be used; but it takes people with spiritual purpose and the beginnings of spiritual experience. Let us remember: everybody was once a beginner, perhaps a very inept beginner. If the will and intention are there, and prayer, God can use you.'[4]

References

1. John L. Casteel, *Spiritual Renewal through Small Groups* (Association Press, NY, 1957), p. 191.
2. Sara K. Little, *Learning Together in the Christian Fellowship* (John Knox Press, U.S.A., 1956), p.31.
3. Lyman Coleman, *Growth by Groups* (Growth by Groups, U.S.A.).
4. Samuel S. Shoemaker, *With the Holy Spirit and with Fire* (Harper & Row, NY, 1960).

Other books consulted—
    R. A. Dow, *Learning through Encounter* (Judson Press, 1971).
    M. Skinner, *House Groups* (Epworth Press & SPCK, 1969).
    Lawrence O. Richards, *69 Ways to Start a Study Group* (Zondervan, 1973.
    Lawrence O. Richards, *A New Face for the Church* (Zondervan, 1970).

12 Evaluating Small Groups

Most of us at one time or another have been members of a group that seemed to get nowhere. Even though the fellowship may have been on a fairly high level the group was not achieving anything really significant. Perhaps the group didn't seem to be functioning properly but it was not clear what was the real problem. Evaluation can help a group appraise the roles people are playing and assess accomplishments.

"The unexamined group life is not worth living".[1] The importance of evaluation to the life of a small group cannot be over-estimated. It is absolutely necessary if the group is to function as a vital activity in which members find fulfilment, significant growth takes place and goals are achieved.

Evaluation will take place whether it is planned or not. Too often evaluation takes place after the meeting by one or two people sharing their frustrations or grievances. The group cannot profit from these private judgements. Only when a group members' critical or reflective comments are heard by the group can something be done about them.

It is a costly activity in terms of time, thought, pride and position, but the benefits far outweigh the costs. It will enrich the participants, individually and as a group. As we evaluate how we are acting in our life together we become increasingly responsible for the life of the total group.

Evaluation of small group life is concerned with understanding what each person is experiencing in that situation. It involves an understanding of the relationships which are taking place, the inter-action between the participants. Group process, just what is actually going on within and between the group members, the series of actions or changes, how the group is operating, is the main concern of evaluation. Based on this evaluation a judgment of what is good and bad can be made. The good can be affirmed, the bad faced and action planned to avoid its continuance. Sometimes the group will feel the need to evaluate "content", the subject matter of the dialogue between the members. Where evaluation has been poor or not undertaken it can result in disturbances and breakdown within the group.

Because human beings are finite and fallible and because the universe of human experience is so complex we will soon discover that there are limitations to our capacities to evaluate. We can easily make incorrect asessments because of our inexperience, our prejudices and the lack of sufficient information. Accordingly we need to adopt an open-minded approach to evaluation. This does not excuse us from making decisions and adjustments based on our evaluation, but it does require us to reserve the right to consider new evidence and adjust to it.

Sara Little suggests four areas in which evaluation should take place at the same time or at different times.

The kind of evaluation necessary

"Purpose — 'Did we achieve our purpose?'

Content — 'What did we learn?'

Group Process — 'How well did we work together?'

Personal Growth — "What happened to us as individuals?' "[2]

She sees values and dangers in each of these aspects. The advantage in evaluating "purpose" is that it links together all that happens in the group in terms of purpose and helps the group keep its purpose before it, continually. The danger is that "over-use may cause the word 'purpose' to lose its meaning."

The advantage of measuring what was learnt **(content)** is that for the group to put into words what they have learned "helps the group organise and clarify its thinking, and have a sense of achievement that something actually *has* been learned." The danger here is that verbalisation cannot always indicate the scope and depth of the learning. Also it can result in "superficial or trite statements which may be a waste of time".

The evaluation of **group process,** Sara Little points out, can be valuable because it engenders greater acceptance of responsibility by all members for what happens. It also helps them develop skills which enable greater group productivity. The danger here is that the group could be so concerned about the process that it becomes an end in itself.

To ask "what happened to us as individuals?" **(Personal Growth),** she says, "Focuses attention on the real purpose behind all study in Christian Fellowship," which is to support and accept each other that all are enabled to grow and mature. The danger is that this can meet with a negative reaction if it is over-used or the group are not ready for it. It also could promote an unhealthy overcover for self or encourage competition.

In the chapter giving guidelines for small groups I emphasized the need for the group to take time out to determine clearly its ultimate (long range) **goals.** Having done this, action or intermediate (short range) goals should be set to give direction to specific periods in the life of the group to enable it to move steadily towards the ultimate purpose for which the group was formed. These goals provide objective criteria against which the accomplishments of the group can be measured. Without this clear statement of purpose no measurement of progress can be made.

Although a mere setting of goals does not ensure their realization or the consequent effectiveness of the group, it is equally true that the group which is heading nowhere will doubtless arrive there! Because the small groups we are dealing with exist as part of the life and mission of the Christian church, goals for small gatherings in the name of Christ, should be consistent with the overall nature and purpose of the wider Christian community.

There are many factors necessary to group effectiveness. We have already listed what Sara Little considers to be the main areas. The following list is not exhaustive but fairly representative. It gives another slant on the kind of evaluation necessary.

1. Clarity of goals
2. Agreement on major and minor goals
3. Agreement on methods of attaining the goals
4. Support of group activities
5. Co-ordination of activities in group tasks
6. Availability of resources necessary for task accomplishment
7. Effectiveness of communication
8. Competence of leadership
9. Clarity of lines of authority
10. Participation in decisions.[3]

This list may be used as a general standard by which to measure the effectiveness of most groups. Sara Little's list and this further listing could be used as the basis for making your own evaluation form or as items for a group to discuss its effectiveness.

Evaluation is an activity in which every group participant should be involved. Opportunity should be given for each member to reflect on their performance and make some attempt at assessing this. The evaluation sheets mentioned later are helpful in this regard. However, this is an entirely subjective evaluation and provision should be made for these sheets to be shared with the whole group. In certain situations it will be wise for the self-evaluation sheets to be kept anonymous and not bear the name of the individuals. This will depend upon the maturity of the individuals and the agreed purpose of the group.

This sharing of individual assessments will give each member an opportunity to participate in the evaluation of the total group life. Other forms may be introduced to further help the members reflect upon the total activity of the group. Samples of these appear later. The lists in the previous section of this chapter as already suggested could be used in this further evaluation. Leadership as well as individual performance will be brought under scrutiny.

There will be an unclassified evaluation that will be continually going on in the mind of **the leader** as he observes the contribution of each member and also seeks to reflect on his own role. From time to time during the meetings a leader will then make an evaluation (and share it with the group) or throw in questions to help the group think about what they are achieving. "That was a helpful contribution from Andrew; Do you agree?" "We seemed to be bogged down here. Any suggestions for a way out?" "I'm getting the feeling that you think this is irrelevant." "Do you think what we are doing is consistent with our purpose?" "Are you finding this helpful?" This role of involving the group in informal evaluation is an important leadership skill.

A member or a specialist can be used to sit outside the group to make an observation about the group's process. If a member is used this gives him or her a new view of the group's life which will be beneficial when he or she rejoins the group. The group will benefit by having someone uninvolved making an evaluation. Where a skilled person who is not a regular member of the group is used as an observer, this gives a high degree of objectivity which is essential for good evaluation. We deal with the role of the observer later.

When to evaluate

Evaluation can be done at some stages during the session but is generally undertaken **after the session** when time is set aside to reflect and determine what experiences have been helpful and what could have been improved.

Occasionally a whole meeting should be given over to do a more thorough evaluation than is possible after most regular meetings. Where a group has met for an experimental period an unhurried time should be allowed for evaluation.

If a **leader's meeting** is held where there is a network of groups, time should be taken out to do some evaluation in each meeting. The outcome of individual group evaluation can be shared especially if unresolved problems have been encountered. In my own experience leaders have found this to be a supportive experience, especially for relatively unskilled leaders.

Each year we held a retreat or non-residential conference to evaluate our multi-cell programmes. These were concerned more with purpose and content although there was consideration of process and growth. All group members completed forms which were collated and used in this annual evaluation.

Ways of evaluating

There is no right method for evaluation. In evaluating Christian group life you will benefit by exploring all of these methods described here. As already mentioned the leader will be involved in informal evaluation continuously. He will observe group members' actions and attitudes to discover anxiety or dissatisfaction. When a member stops attending he will follow-up to discover why and not be easily put off by evasive explanations. The behaviour of members in the group clearly reveals disinterest or disagreement. A question to the persons concerned during or after the group can bring to the surface issues which the whole group can evaluate.

A natural way to evaluate which doesn't give the appearance of a structured evaluation is simply to ask the group at the end of the meeting — "What did you like best?" "What did you like least?" "What was most helpful?" This method of **general discussion** within the group seems to be a low key approach but can result in some in-depth assessment. The leader will need to be a free person who is willing and able to accept suggestions without becoming defensive.

Another way is to use **reaction sheets** or check lists. These require time for completion by individuals, collation and discussion. Generally 30 to 45 minutes is needed but when the group becomes skilled in this method less time is required. Following a brief explanation by the leader they are completed and handed in unsigned to allow for an honest expression of feelings. (Names may be recorded on the sheets in special circumstances, as mentioned previously.)

After completion they are collected and redistributed to other members. Where applicable, ratings are tabulated and totals recorded. A chart can be used to list the totals for the group. On sheets where written answers are required the items are taken one at a time with each member reading out the comment on the sheet before him. Invariably a wide range of opinion will be shown. This diversity of feeling and opinion generally sparks off a lively discussion. There will be no one right answer so all honest expressions of feeling count and should be considered.

A further method of conducting evaluation is to **use an observer.** An observer may be a group member, or a person from outside the group who has special skills in this area. The observer sits outside the group noting and recording how the group works. A record is kept of what is observed about how the group functions concerning process and the taking of responsibility. The observer is generally concerned with performance rather than the subject-matter (content) of the discussion. In certain instances the content is also observed. The observer may be called upon for comment by the group while it is still operating but generally the observations are fed in at the conclusion of the group. These observations help to hold a mirror up to the group to show it how it is working. We deal with this method in more detail later in the chapter.

A tape or cassette **recording of the session** is another method of evaluating. At the conclusion of the discussion the tape is played back, members making notes of what they learnt about the group's performance. This is followed by a comparison of notes and discussion. A variation is to get everyone to identify their own voice and place a tick on a paper each time they hear themselves speak. The totals of each person's participation are shared and the individuals discuss what they learned about the degree and manner of their own performance.

This method can lose interest if a long session has to be replayed. Ten minutes playback may be sufficient before attention wanes.

A way of evaluation which can be passed off by the average group all too quickly is to use video equipment. This equipment is more readily available than most realize. There are Video Centres in all capital cities, and many provincial centres, provided by the government, where this equipment is available. Training is offered by the Centres. Many educational and commercial institutions in the community are also willing to make video equipment available, providing it is accompanied by a qualified operator.

Video taping offers the advantages of allowing participants to see as well as hear how they functioned. Facial expressions, gestures, posture, all provide additional significant information. The prejudices and limitations of a human observer affect the feed-back to the group whereas the video is entirely unselective, apart from the focussing of the camera operator.

Types of evaluation or reaction sheets
There are a number of types of reaction sheets. Some are for self-evaluation by each individual of the manner in which they functioned. Others are concerned with the way in which the group worked as a whole. Some use general questions, others contrasting statements, and some use open-ended statements.

Frequently alert members will question certain phrases in a checklist and rightly so. If this is the case have the group create its own. It will make the evaluation more meaningful to the group.

Here are samples of the different types of sheets mentioned.

General Questions:
What was our purpose as you saw it?
Did we achieve the purpose?
Why or why not?

Another grouping:
What did you particularly like about this meeting?
What did you particularly dislike?

or: What were the strong points of today's session?
What were the weak points?
What improvements would you suggest for the future?
Another set of questions could be:
What did you like best about the session?
What did you like least about the session?
What will be most useful to you?
What did you learn from the session today?
What specific things came up today that you would have liked to explore further?
How would you suggest the session could have been improved?

Contrasting Statements:

Instructions: Circle one of the five points on the scale which most nearly represents your reaction in relation to the contrasting statements at each end of the scale.

How did you like the session today?

| Excellent | 5 | 4 | 3 | 2 | 1 | Poor |

Were the purposes clear?

| Very clear | 5 | 4 | 3 | 2 | 1 | Not Clear |

How well did the group work together?

| Very well | 5 | 4 | 3 | 2 | 1 | Poorly |

How did you feel as a member of the group?

| Accepted | 5 | 4 | 3 | 2 | 1 | Rejected |

How did you feel that the subject matter was presented?

| Very well | 5 | 4 | 3 | 2 | 1 | Poorly |

How did you feel about participating in the discussion?

| Very free | 5 | 4 | 3 | 2 | 1 | Very inhibited |

How interested were you in the topic?

| Very interested | 5 | 4 | 3 | 2 | 1 | Not at all interested |

Did you gain any new ideas or insights about the problem?

| Many | 5 | 4 | 3 | 2 | 1 | None |

How suitable was the method of teaching?

| Very suitable | 5 | 4 | 3 | 2 | 1 | Not at all suitable |

How relaxed did you feel?

| Completely relaxed | 5 | 4 | 3 | 2 | 1 | Extremely tense |

There is a useful check list for evaluating Christian group life using contrasting statements in *Church Meetings that Matter* by Philip A. Anderson, on pages 50 to 52 which "may be reproduced without permission by local churches for use in Christian small group meetings".

Open-ended Questions:
Reactions to what happened in the session:
The most helpful thing that happened to me today was

Today it would have been helpful if someone

Considering the things that people did today, I tended to admire

Our progress was hindered today when
I was somewhat surprised at
It was disappointing when
It was encouraging to me when
I felt uncomfortable when
I had a comfortable feeling when
I had a feeling of disapproval when
I had a feeling of approval when

Questions for Self Evaluation:
An example of questions for self evaluation are given by Sara Little who suggests they be used for **occasional** use by the group of members. This is not a formal questionnaire but covers the areas of responsibility that the members should have toward the functioning of the group.
— Did I prepare before I came, both by prayer and study?
— Did I really try to listen to every person and understand exactly what he/she was saying?
— Did I monopolize the conversation? Or, when I spoke did I have something relevant to contribute or a question to ask that helped us to move along in our thinking?
— Did I make any effort to help when I saw something was needed — either a question or a fact or a response to some person? Or did I just feel critical and do nothing?
— Was I honest? Or, did I say what I thought the group expected?
— Did I make an effort to think and speak clearly, and to listen to others expectantly, believing that

God can and does speak through us to one another?
— Am I willing to follow through on implications for myself of any truth I glimpsed? Or, do I see only what it means for someone else?

Other questions which could be used for self evaluation are:

— I feel that I understand myself better.
— I am more comfortable about expressing my feelings.
— I learned to express my feelings more accurately.
— I think I know people in this group quite a bit better than before.
— I learned that there is a lot more to most people than I usually take account of.
— I'm better at knowing how others really feel.
— I think perhaps I can be a little freer in my behaviour toward others after this experience.
— I learned how complicated and difficult leadership can be.
— I learned something about how I come across to others.
— I learned to accept other people's feelings about me without being too defensive or "taking it personally".

These questions could be listed on sheets with three or four columns next to them in which individuals check their response. The columns for the first set could be headed: Not at All. A Little. Fairly Much. Very Much.

The columns for the second set could be headed: No Opinion. No Growth. Little Growth. Much Growth.

The findings in these personal check lists may be shared with the group. However, this will need to be a group decision. Keep it optional for people to share these with the assurance that any may dissent without being thought less of by the rest of the group.

Observers

Group observers play an important role in helping groups improve their effectiveness. They make it possible for objectivity in evaluation to the degree that is not possible when members involved as participants seek to evaluate the group in most of the ways with which we have already dealt. The observer is the eyes of the group, and the ears as well, listening for pertinence, frequency and interaction of the contributors. The observer is the historian of the group's life for a brief period. The observer helps the group see itself.

The observer sits outside the group in a position where what is going on can be observed. The observer may change his position occasionally to observe the facial expressions of some members. He or she does not break into the group discussion or make any side comments. However, the group may call on the observer for a report at certain points in the session. Usually this report is given at the end of the session.

Being an observer is an interesting and enjoyable experience during which one learns about the dynamics of group life. For this reason over a period each member of the group should be given the opportunity to fulfill this role.

The following are some **tips for observers:**

— Make sure you understand your role clearly. If using a check list, be conversant with the items it lists.

— Don't disturb the group by unnecessary movement or noise.

— Do not sit too close to the group. You will be able to observe all that is taking place from a position two or three metres away.

— Make notes that will help you recall your observations. So much happens so fast.

In reporting back to the group keep in mind these points:

— Be sensitive to what information the group is ready to use — what will be most helpful to the group now rather than what was the most interesting point observed.

— Don't be dogmatic. Remember that your report is one person's observations. This will always be affected by your values and perspective.

— Don't avalanche the group with information. If too much is given it can't be used. Select observations that will stimulate thinking and discussion. Let the group ask for more information as they need it.

— Don't praise the group too much. Learning doesn't take place by being told only pleasant things. Mentioning accomplishments is desirable if it helps the group face difficulties honestly and constructively.

— Don't fix blame or preach or judge. The observer's role is not that of evaluator, expert and judge, but is that of questioner and fact-giver. He or she says, "My record shows that four people have not participated so far; Is that desirable?" He or she does not say, "John and Mary are dominating the discussion". The observer may use other questions and comments like these: "It appeared to me that you bogged down at this point . . .". "Why do you think this was so . . .?" "It seemed to me that this could have been a contributing factor . . ." "What do you think?" "Why didn't someone break in?" "Were you all satisfied with the decision?" "Did June have some special reason for . . .?" "I wonder how Graham felt when Paul and Matthew started . . .?"

— Do not emphasize personality clashes. It is usually better to discuss what helped and what hindered the whole group.

We have found it helpful to use **two observers** at the one time. One uses a chart to record the pattern of verbal interaction in the group. The other makes notes based on a series of questions which form a suggested "Check list".

The observer using the **chart** places a large piece of chart paper in the centre of the group and each person with a texta draws a small circle on the chart to represent their position, writing their name next to it. We find this "personalizes" the chart. One observer sits outside the circle and charts the interaction by drawing a line from the name of the speaker to the name of the one he seems to be speaking to. Remarks addressed to the group in general go to the centre of the circle. As the lines accumulate they will show who speaks the most and silent members will stand out clearly. The drawing will look something like this:

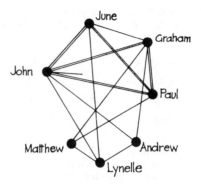

During the report segment the chart is placed in the centre of the group in the same position as it was previously. The discussion could centre around these questions:

— How do the group members feel about the amount of their participation?
— Has anyone dominated the discussion?
— How do people feel about getting, or not getting, attention?
— What can be done to gain wider participation?

The other observer observes the group with the aid of the following **check-list** which covers the main things that the observer should look for and note. We have found most observers need a short time at the conclusion of the session to complete their reports. However, it should be made clear that the observer is not to read the report but draw the group into discussion with appropriate questions. Where an observer is unskilled he may feed in his observations one point at a time and the leader involves the group in discussion. Another way for the new observer to present his report is to ask the group the questions listed on his check-list and after a brief reaction from the group, give his own observations.

Suggested Check List for Observers

This is a sample only. Feel free to modify it for your situation.

1. **Purpose**
   (a) Is the purpose of the group clear?....................
   (b) Is there a clear understanding of the function of the group by members?...........................
   ....If not, why not?...........................

   (c) What is the aim of the group?.............. ....
   ....

2. **General Atmosphere**
   (a) Is there an informal, friendly atmosphere?...........
   (b) Or is it formal and tense?...........................
   (c) Do members feel free to say what they think?........
   (d) How well do the members listen to one another?
   ....

3. **The Leader**
   (a) Is the leader able to direct and guide his group satisfactorily?...........................

   (b) Did he lose control of the meeting at any time? Why?...........................
   (c) Does the leader dictate to the group?...............
   ....Why?...........................
   (d) Was the meeting too rigid in form?...................
   Why?...........................
   (e) Is the leader sensitive to group needs?.............
   ....
   (f) Is he concerned only with the topic?..................
   ....

4. **Participation**
   (a) Do most of the members take part in the discussion?...........................
   (b) To what extent are they really involved rather than being a captive audience?...................
   ....

   (c) Are some of the leadership functions shared by group members?...........................
   (d) To what extent are they achieving shared leadership?...........................
   ....

5. **Other Comments**

References

1. Philip A. Anderson, *Church Meetings that Matter* (United Church Press) p. 58.
2. Sara Little, *Learning Together in the Christian Fellowship* (John Knox Press, 1956), p. 60.
3. D. Cartwright and A. Zander, *Group Dynamics Research and Theory*, (Row, Peterson and Company).

   Other books consulted:
   Harold D. Munar, *Techniques and Resources for Guiding Adult Groups* (Abingdon).
   Beth and Frances Strauss, *New Ways to Better Meetings* (Viking).

13   Evangelism and Outreach through Small Groups

Small groups are one way to undertake evangelism. They are not the only way — large groupings still have a very significant role to play. We need to explore a great variety of approaches to evangelism and use as many as possible. The small group is one visible form which is being extensively used. But it is more than just an effective tool.

One of the best brief discussions of evangelism I have seen recently is that by Athol Gill, "What is Evangelism" in *Youth Outreach and Evangelism,* (The Joint Board of Christian Education of Australia and New Zealand 1975).

In an assessment of evangelism and mission in the New Testament he points out that there was:

> "no uniform approach to mission and evangelism during the New Testament period. As in all other areas of life and thought there was a variety of approaches and there were significant differences among the various churches" (p.10).

In his examination of the church's recovery of its sense of mission he says:

> "The evangelistic programmes which will probably command most respect will be those which treat the hearers as persons and respect their integrity, which are able to meet them at the point of their present understanding, **which encourage long-term in-depth involvement with them**, which take place primarily out in the world as an integral part of the total ongoing ministry of the Christian community, which readily incorporate new Christians into that ministry and contribute to its spiritual development". (p. 15, our emphasis)

Robert A. Raines writes[1]:

> **"It is the main task of the church to provide the conditions and circumstances in which God may awaken people or reawaken them.** Church leaders must learn how to prepare people for conversion. We must lead our people into those places where the wind blows, where the Holy Spirit is working. It is this writer's conviction that the most propitious conditions for awakening prevail in koinonia groups centering on Bible study."

Some advantages of small groups as a basis for evangelism

— **They offer a bridge for shy people** — who may be painfully uncomfortable in crowds or large groups or who may be wary of church and church buildings.

— **They are personal** — one person in a crowd may be very lonely and feel very insignificant. In a small group that person will respond to the group's care and concern, and to the group's recognition of his identity and worth.

— **A small group allows maximum participation.** Each person has the opportunity to ask questions, to participate in the discussion and to share ideas and feelings.

— **They are flexible.** The length, time and venue of the meeting can be varied and the programme need not be fixed in a definite pattern.

— **There is a minimum or organisation needed**

— **Evangelism is localised** — A home is identified with the Gospel in a neighbourhood.

— **They encourage spontaneity in evangelism.**

— **They are informal** — a relaxed, natural atmosphere is possible.

— **Communication is easier** — In the small group situation personal problems may be shared and solutions, both practical and theoretical, can be offered. We may be able to present the Christian message more easily and clearly. Difficulties can be discussed and problems clarified, knowledge can be shared. The small group offers a very natural situation in which we can share our personal Christian experience.

Friendship/Contact Groups

Purpose These groups are intended to make a contact with irregular church attenders and the unchurched. They are concerned with creating a situation in which bridges of friendship can be commenced. They hopefully lay a foundation upon which deeper communication can take place at a later stage. They offer a hand of friendship which can be accepted or refused without the person being rejected. They are reaching in love to touch other peoples' lives. They are non-threatening situations where the people invited determine the degree to which they wish to be involved. The programme is essentially of a 'getting acquainted nature. They provide a climate in which the Holy Spirit can work to the extent He chooses.

Who to invite

(a) **Where the group is part of a local church programme** — In keeping with the purpose of these groups, the majority of those invited will be unchurched or irregular attenders.

Those invited will probably be restricted to those in some way associated with the sponsoring church.

Another couple who are closely aligned with the church should be invited to share the organization and conduct the group. But be careful to choose those who have real sensitivity and relate well to those outside the church.

(b) **Where the group is not part of a local church programme** — Where a couple are seeking to reach out to their immediate neighbourhood. No neighbours should be omitted from being on the invitation list (Be optimistic, some of the most unlikely people may respond.)

It will still be helpful to have another committed couple, of the type described above, sharing in the experience.

(c) **Inviting families** — There is an advantage in having families involved together in these experiences. However, the age and interest of the children and young people will determine whether modifications need to be made to the programme. Generally a buffet or barbecue type meal together provides a relaxed informal atmosphere and natural groupings of the various ages.

An alternative programme for the children or young people will allow the adults and other youth to relate in an undisturbed atmosphere.

(d) **Social groups for youth** — The invitations will be similar to those for adults with a number of committed youth being present.

One parish conducted these groups after school. A

number of young people invited some of their friends from school who had been asking questions about the Christian faith. The groups were held in the minister's loungeroom.

How to invite

Generally, the best invitation is a personal one. However, there is some advantage in sending a hand-written (or printed) invitation and following this up with a personal visit, as this gives opportunity for the invitation to be discussed prior to the personal contact.

Be sure to state clearly the purpose of the meeting. To simply call it a purely social evening to get to know each other is possibly the best way to describe it.

State clearly the time for conclusion (as well as the time for commencement).

How many to invite

Ideally twelve (with a maximum of 16) people make the best number for this type of group. This allows reasonable opportunity for participation by each person and permits those who don't want to get involved too much not to be too obvious.

Usually more have to be invited than will actually attend. Less than eight in this type of group does not allow the group to function satisfactorily.

Venue

Usually contact groups are held in private homes. Halls or rooms in church halls are too impersonal and can be threatening to those who are not used to attending church regularly. The hosts should be warm hospitable people and their homes need to be clean and tidy.

When to hold these groups

Generally these are held in the mornings or afternoons during the week if they are intended to reach women or retired folk only. For couples, Sunday morning after church, on Sunday afternoon, or any evening have been successful. Saturday evenings seem to be a convenient time for family barbecues. Youth seem to prefer after school for high-schoolers, or Friday and Saturday evenings.

Preparation

Name-tags for each person should be prepared beforehand. They are helpful for group fellowship and assist the leadership. The lettering should be ½" to ¾" high so that it can be read at a distance. Ashtrays should be readily available without people having to ask for them. Seating should be arranged to enable each member to see the rest of the group. Light background music could be playing as the guests arrive. But don't use "religious" music. Supper or morning tea should be set up beforehand to prevent disturbing the meeting.

Programme

Introduce people as they come, give them name tags and allow time for informal conversations.

Use one of the get-acquainted games in the "Games" booklet. The Interview Game is a non-threatening game. The questions can be varied to suit those who attend. Don't use questions which probe, e.g., What is your aim in life? Keep them general at this stage. The "Guess Who Fishbowl" is helpful for those who know each other well. Again, watch the questions you choose. (You will need small cheap note pads and pencils.)

Well chosen and well presented slides make a good focus for an evening. The host can show his own slides on an interesting topic. A variation is to invite the participants to each bring 12 or so of their best slides and present them. If you wish to get variety ask them to bring a few family slides, a few of a happy experience, some showing the beauty of the world and one or two funny slides.

Serve supper or refreshments. Finish on time. Allow plenty of time for informal conversation during supper.

Some hints

— Listen carefully to people. Show a real interest in them.
— Be alert to expressions of need — whatever they may be
  — physical, emotional, spiritual, etc. Follow up on these.
— Don't be easily shocked by what some may say.
— Avoid controversial subjects.
— Be natural.
— Don't be surprised if people want to talk about spiritual matters. Be sensitive to the desire of the whole group to pursue these matters.
— Don't limit the work of the Holy Spirit. His purpose for the group might go well beyond what you intended originally.
— Pray about the meeting beforehand and ask others to support you also.
— "Live at the centre" yourself so you will be available and usable. Your own close communion with God will be your best preparation.

189

Evangelistic Encounter Groups

These groups could be part of a more structured local church small group programme such as Lay Witness Teams Missions (see *Lay Witness Teams* by John Mallison) or Dialogue Evangelism (material available from Anglican Diocese of Sydney, Dept. of Evangelism).

However, the more spontaneous groups being considered here will come into being and function in a similar manner to the Contact Groups. Generally they will happen because of the love and concern of a small number of Christian disciples for those who have not made a commitment to Christ.

Unlike Friendship/Contact Groups, these have a specific aim to present the Christian Good News, with its call to faith in Christ. When people are invited to such groups it should be made clear that the group will seek to explore seriously the meaning of the Christian faith for today.

Some Programme Ideas

— Use a 'get acquainted' game.

— For the **main segment** consider one of the following:

— Use a speaker on a theme of general interest who gives a Christian perspective on such issues as "Understanding and Helping Teenagers", "Family or Marriage Enrichment", "Children", "Coping with Crises", etc. Follow with question time and discussion.

— Use a well-presented Christian film or an audio-visual (a filmstrip with recorded commentary) on a subject of interest to the group. Check the titles the Australian Religious Film Society, Scripture Union, Challenge Films and Gospel Film Ministry have available. Follow with question time and discussion.

— Give a copy of the same book to each person a few weeks prior to the meeting. Ask them to read it and be prepared to discuss their reaction to the book. Some authors to consider would be Keith Miller, Bruce Larson, Tom Skinner, David Wilkerson, Michael Green, Catherine Marshall, and Eugenia Price.

— Use a sensitive Christian speaker who can give a concise, illustrated talk on some aspect of the Christian gospel. Allow time for discussion.

— Use a suitable cassette recording or a record. There are numbers available from Christian bookshops and cassette libraries. The Creative Resources cassettes produced by Word and available through Gospel Film Ministry in Australia include a broad cross-section of subjects and well-known speakers and writers.

— Invite one or two sensitive people who have a vital up-to-date Christian experience and can express themselves reasonably well. These can be invited to share the story of their experience of God's grace at work in their lives. (This witnessing needs to be specific.) The meeting is then thrown open for the group to react.

Alternatively, the leader could interview the witnesses using questions such as the following:

— For how long have you had a meaningful faith?

— How did you find this faith?

— What helped you make this discovery?

— What prevented you from making it earlier?

— What difference did it make at first?

— How is it working out in specific situations in daily living?

— See *Lay Witness Teams* by John Mallison for an effective inductive method involving guest witnesses and the whole group.

Some hints

— Be prepared with some suitable booklets for those who wish to make commitments or think more about what was said.

— Be available to people immediately after the group or at other times outside the group.

— Take a long-term view—follow up people who showed interest (and those who did not appear to!).

— Prepare for the group with prayer.

Reference:

1. Robert A. Raines, *New Life in the Church* (Harper & Row, New York, 1961).

14   Nurture in Small Groups

Unfortunately, the Christian church has not always been faithful in its care of new disciples. It has preached the Good News and tried to win people to Christ and rejoiced when people have come to faith in Jesus Christ but often those who have responded have not been properly cared for. Like new-born human babies, those who are "born anew" spiritually need special care to help them become established.

Why small groups for nurture?

The church must create a climate of supportive fellowship for all associated with it. A community offering genuine care and concern needs to be developed. A new disciple must be helped to understand that re-generation is not an individualistic relationship with God, occurring in isolation from others. Regeneration **into** the body of Christ is an essential part of the Gospel. But the new believer needs to experience the body of Christ in microcosm, to have an in-depth experience of all that is involved in real Christian fellowship.

Small face to face groups, for the nurture of those who have responded in faith to the proclamation of the Gospel provide an effective means of helping new disciples reorientate themselves to their new Christian style of life. They provide in miniature a representation of what the Christian church is called to be. They can also be the ideal bridge to the total life and fellowship of the local Christian community.

The **nurture group** can be described as the "nursery" which adjoins the "labour ward" (**the evangelistic group**). The evangelistic group seeks to bring forth new life, to help people to be "born" spiritually. The nurture group exists to help establish that new life. It is not only a nursery for new-born babes; it is also the "kindergarten" group. Teaching will include instruction in just what takes place when a person responds to Christ in faith. Simple basic concepts of the Christian faith are introduced and some guidance is given in how to live the Christian life.

In my parish ministry I found the new disciples nurture group to be one of the most important small groups we organised. People who indicated, in one way or another, that they had made an initial commitment to Christ were invited with others to a small short term group in my home. Many indicated that this nurture experience made a vital contribution in helping them become established in their new found faith.

"Really the whole problem of giving personal care to every believer is only resolved in a thorough understanding of the nature and mission of the church. It is well here to observe that the emergence of the church principle around Jesus, whereby one believer was brought into fellowship with others, was the practice in a larger dimension of the same thing that He was doing with the Twelve. One cannot help but observe in this connection that the references to "the disciples" as a corporate body are much more frequent in the Gospels than are references to an individual disciple (One commentator contends that) most of the references to individuals refer to failures on their part, while the references to the group as a whole more often speak of their joy, understanding or achievement". (Coleman, p. 46.)

"There is simply no substitute for getting with people, and it is ridiculous to imagine that anything less, short of a miracle, can develop strong Christian leadership. After all, if Jesus, the Son of God, found it necessary to stay almost constantly with His few disciples for three years, and even one of them was lost, how can a church expect to do this job on an assembly line basis a few days out of the year?" (Coleman, p. 48.)

When to hold nurture groups

The new disciple should be invited to share in a nurture group experience as soon as possible after his commitment. When a local church is planning an outreach project the structure for the nurture groups should be set up at the same time as the outreach is being planned, to permit an immediate follow-up programme. Churches frequently neglect making these plans in advance, resulting in a time delay in which valuable contact is not available when the new disciple is in need of support and encouragement.

The local church which is active in outreach and which does not depend upon occasional evangelistic events will need to be alert to the continuing need to provide nurture group experiences to support new members.

Who should initiate?

In an active local church nurture groups will be seen as an integral part of the Christian community life. Some churches appoint a person to supervise this aspect of the pastoral care programme. This person has the authority to initiate new groups to meet immediate needs.

Where the new disciples are young people the youth leader should take the initiative in establishing a nurture group.

If the local congregation has an active small group programme, the small group leaders' meeting could be assigned the responsibility for a small group nurture programme which would be linked with the continuing growth groups.

Where none of the above structures exist, a minister may take the initiative but there is room in every church for mature Christians to take the lead in offering themselves for this task.

The important thing is that the new life is nurtured and consolidated, especially in the early stages.

Where should the group be held?

A home is the obvious venue, because of the intimacy and warmth which it provides. There is an advantage in holding these short-term orientation meetings in the home of the minister or pastor. This links the person with the "spiritual leader" of the church and can help in assuring him of an open door to further help and friendship.

If the home of a "lay minister" is to be used, the hosts should be warm, sensitive people who are held in high regard by the local church members.

Who to invite?

In addition to the new disciples, invite a few other members of the local church to provide a link with some of the caring fellowship. If the person who has made a commitment is married, the partner should be invited too. Young people can be invited to bring a companion, if they wish. Youth leaders and other committed young people will be invited where those to be nurtured are young people.

How long should nurture groups run?

The type of group envisaged here is a short-term cell which exists long enough to guide the new Christians into their style of life. They should then be channelled into a continuing growth group. If there is no overall small group programme the nurture group may itself develop into the growth group.

Some nurture groups meet for one or two sessions

before graduating the newcomer to the growth group. Others have met for six months or more. Perhaps a church which has a number of new disciples seeking membership might consider running an adult education programme, linked with a shepherding-nurture group. Graduates of this programme could join growth groups.

In a caring fellowship all new disciples are usually **How to invite** assigned a "sponsor" or "spiritual guardian" who follows them up personally after their commitment. This person acts as an "extension of the everlasting arms", befriending, supporting, encouraging and helping them become established. Theirs is an important role. It may involve helping a previously unchurched person with the most basic spiritual issues. They will accompany such a person to the worship of the gathered church and introduce them to its members. Such a person will be the obvious one to invite and accompany the newcomer to the nurture group. In a situation where such support is not offered, the pastor or lay ministers will invite people personally to the group. Invitations should always be by word of mouth.

— It is important new disciples have a good experience of **What help** a real caring, concerned Christian community where they **should be** will feel accepted and significant. Do everything you can **given?** to make the meetings of the group, times for experiencing true Christian love. Make sure everyone feels welcome and be sure all get to know each other. Use some get acquainted 'games' (see Book 2). Spend time in praise and worship.

— Keep the meetings interesting. Avoid long talks by the leader. Use visual aids (even if only diagrams on a chalk board). Encourage questions and allow time for sharing.

— **Keep it simple** and don't swamp them with too much information or take-home material in any one session.

— Be aware that many will not know very much about the Christian faith and how to live it. Most will not know how to read their Bibles or how to pray. Focus on 'the how' not 'the ought'.

— Show the Christian life as a long road—a day by day growing experience.

— Help them understand and grow in their new relationship to God (as Father, Son and Holy Spirit), to themselves, to others and to the world.

— Have more mature sensitive Christians share with them in the group.

— Teach them how to share their faith with sensitivity. Emphasize the importance of life-style and taking time to make genuine friendships with people.

— Arrange some opportunities for informal social get-togethers to help them get to know each other and their families.

The First Nurture Group Meeting

— Have copies of Bibles and systematic Bible reading programmes, such as Scripture Union or I.B.R.A. available for them to inspect and purchase.

— Have simple books on prayer and Christian living available for them to borrow or purchase, such as: "Teach Us to Pray" by W. E. Sangster, "Understanding the Way" by Robinson and Winward, and "New Life, New Lifestyle" by Michael Green.

— Allow plenty of time for a general sharing time. This will play an important role in helping the new disciples build confidence in expressing their faith. Ask some of the following questions of the whole group and let individuals respond at will. Encourage shy members to share but don't force them.

— Can you think of one word to describe how you felt when you made your commitment?

— What impressed you most about the meeting where you made your commitment?

— What helped you make this step?

— What prevented you from making it earlier?

— How is it working out?

— What help do you need to enable you to grow?

— Give an illustrated talk explaining again the steps in making a commitment of one's life to Jesus Christ. It is important that they clearly understand what they have done. Also, cover what is involved now in living out their new Christian life. Introduce the means by which God's grace can be experienced (prayer, Bible study, worship, fellowship and obedience to God's intention for them).

Be sure to help them understand that God, the Holy Spirit, now lives within—they no longer have to live in their own strength—it is a life shared with God.

— The above may need to be spread over a few meetings.

— **Suggested programme** for the first session:
    — Get acquainted session (using a 'game'—see Book 2)
    — Praise (sing two or three hymns or songs used in the meetings where the commitments were made)
    — Brief prayer segment
    — Talk and discussion
    — General sharing time
    — Introduction of aids for growth on display (Bibles, books, etc.)
    — Praise
    — Supper.

Reference:

1. Robert E. Coleman, *The Master Plan of Evangelism* (Revell, 1964).

15   'At Home' Groups

This outline is based on the experience of the author with a number of "At Homes" held at Liverpool, Hamilton and Port Kembla Uniting Parishes. In each instance many favourable comments were received from the participants. Such remarks usually concerned the pleasure of being invited to meet socially in the minister's home, and the opportunity to get to know other members of the congregation better. In one of the above situations two elderly church members who had been attending the same church for forty years, confessed that the evening provided the first experience of conversing with each other beyond a merely formal short greeting after Sunday worship!

This form of small group has now been tried in other areas by some who have participated in Small Groups Conferences where the concept was introduced.

While at Bega Uniting Parish, the minister, Rev. Ross Kingham, reported: "We have found 'At Home' groups very effective in our area. Within a three-week period we were able to meet 180 folk in this way. Being a rural area, not all folk could travel easily to our home in Bega. Therefore, five meetings were held in our home, with three others being held in private homes in the outlying centres. These have been held to integrate newcomers to the parish as well as to assist us in getting to know the established congregation.

"New folk have deeply appreciated the experience of acceptance and warmth that such an evening provides. They participate in one or two relationship games and talk informally over supper. By this means those who are either new to the area, or who have lived in the locality for some time but without feeling incorporated in a congregation, are helped to link up with others. Another interesting and unexpected by-product of these evenings has been the genuine uplift given to the 'older' members doing the welcoming. A number of these folk have stated later that they were thankful for what the evening had meant to them in terms of personal satisfaction and enjoyment, and knowing they had been able to minister to others."

Rev. Dieter Tieman, when ministering at Albion Park Rail, reported: "We followed your outline almost to the letter and found it to be most effective. Over a period of 12 nights we had 164 different people attend our home. Sub-committees were formed in each of the three centres in the parish to undertake the organization necessary. The church ladies supplied the supper for each evening.

"We followed your suggestion to use a set of slides. About 40 to 50 of general interest were shown. These had something to do with our personal experience, places we had visited and tasks we have undertaken. The best groups were between 15 and 18 people. These evenings were a tremendous strain on the whole family, but looking back, we feel it was well worth while. We now plan to hold further groups in the future."

Aims

An "At Home" function has three aims:
1. To help the congregation to get to know the minister **and his wife.**
2. To help the minister **and his wife** get to know as many of the congregation as they can in a **short** period of time.
3. To help the congregation get to know each other better.

When to hold "At Homes"

"At Homes" provide an effective way to get to know a large number of people in a relatively short period. For that reason they are useful when a minister moves to a new appointment to help him get to know his people quickly. However, they have been used by the writer later during his ministry in the same parish with equally good effect. In this case the programme was varied from that used in the original series.

It was the writer's practice to use this type of group on a continuing basis to help orient newcomers. In this case names of new arrivals were recorded and when two or three couples were listed, invitations were sent. A number of members of the congregation were also invited to help the newcomers integrate into the local church community.

Organisation

It is essential that the minister and his wife **do not** get involved in the tedious details of the actual organisation. If the plan outlined here is followed, the minister will be heavily committed in the demanding visitation programme and his wife will be busy hosting the meetings in addition to her normal schedule.

A small group of people with a good knowledge of the local church people should handle the organisation. (These need not necessarily be church office-bearers; they could be a small group already in existence, such as a women's Bible Study group). It can be explained that the minister and his wife will be busy in the "at home" programme and wish to concentrate on getting to know people rather than getting involved with the details of organisation.

Organising Committee's duties

1. **Make master list**
   — The group compile an up-to-date master list of people including all who have some connection with the church.
   — Information can be drawn from the Sunday School Roll, Youth Group membership lists, Church Membership Roll, Women's and Men's Groups.
   — The list is graded into 'actives' and 'inactives'.
   — The list is divided into areas and then into streets (in order of street number).

Note: The minister does a crash-visitation programme — this method of listing enables a systematic house-to-house visitation.

2. **Make Groupings**
   — The list is divided into groups of 25. It has been found that 25-30 people need to be invited at one time to ensure an attendance of 12-15. However, this varies from place to place.

— Each group should contain a proportion of 'actives' and 'inactives' (say 2/3 'inactives' and 1/3 'actives').
— These smaller groups are still kept in areas and in street order.
— It may be found advisable to include some special groups, e.g. for young married couples and young people.

3. Prepare group lists
— The group lists should be typed on loose-leaf sheets which fit into a small folder.
— One page per group, three copies of each list.
(One copy is the minister's visitation list,
One copy is kept near the minister's phone to record phone replies, and one copy is filed.)

Layout:

....		Other Info.
(Date of "At Home")	Code	(Family details,
Name Address	'A' or 'InA'	positions held, etc.)

4. Enlist 'Actives' to help
— The Organising Committee contact 'Actives' in each of the groups to bring supper and help with the washing-up.

5. Prepare and post invitations
— The invitation should be printed, preferably in script, leaving a blank space for the name of the people invited and the date. They should be of a size which will fold easily into a standard envelope.

Wording:
The Rev. John and Mrs. Everyman invite you
to be their guests at an informal social evening
in their home on ....
commencing at .... p.m.
Supper will be served at .... p.m.
To assist with catering arrangements, we would
 appreciate it if we could have a reply by ....
(one week in advance).
174 Pilgrims Way,
Southaven, 2999.
Tel. 174-2999.

— Names and addresses should be typed on envelopes, which are then stamped.
— Keep in batches with dates on front of each bundle.
— Post invitations four to five weeks before date of each "At Home".
— One person on the committee should be responsible for the regular mailing of the invitations.
— Encourage replies by mail to prevent excessive phone calls.

Notes:

If possible, use the rectory or manse, even if it is not a very large house.

If this really isn't feasible, use homes of key members.

If people cannot come to an "At Home" and let you know, fit in an additional "At Home" for them.

Launching

Announce to the Parish Council/Session your intention to hold "At Homes". Point out that these functions are to have priority over your other activities (for example, no Scripture teaching in schools during the three-month period).

Announce to the Congregation — tell them that everyone will be invited at some time.

Work out dates of the "At Homes" well in advance, and give them to the Organising Committee.

Visitation

— Visit by lists, whether a reply has been received or not.
— Call one week before the "At Home".
— Make the call brief. Introduce yourself as the minister. Mention invitation (you may find you will be picking up replies). Express a hope that they might be able to share in this 'informal social evening'.
— Call even if people have said they will not be coming to the "At Home".
— If no-one is home, leave your card with a note.

The evening

Notes: Have name tags prepared (in large print so that they may be able to be read from across the room). Be ready well in advance, introduce people as they come and allow informal conversation.

— State aims of the evening.

— Play the 'get-acquainted' game ("Interviews").

— Generally, a programme of slides has been presented. This should last no longer than 30 minutes and be fast moving. This could includes slides relating to your own life, college training, marriage, children, some highlights of past ministeries and slides of general interest. This could give insight into your own background and interests and build confidence as people learn of the experience which you are bringing to the new situation.

— Supper.

— Brief 'family' prayer.

— Finish on time.

"Interview" — Get Acquainted Game:

Re-arrange group so that husband and wife are not interviewing each other. Questions are listed on large chart or roneoed sheet. Each person is given pencil and paper and they interview the person next to them. Interviews take two minutes. Each then reverse their role and interview the other person for a similar period. On completion each interviewer introduces his neighbour to the group.

The minister and his wife participate in this.

Questions:

— Name?

— Where do you live?

— How long have you been living in the area?

— Where did you live when you were 10 years of age?

— Family

— Special interests — hobbies, sport, clubs

— Occupation

— Positions in church

— What was the nicest thing that happened to you in the last 12 months?

Note: If people say they would like to come but cannot get a baby-sitter, perhaps it would be possible to have the Organising Committee make arrangements for this.

Immediately after the meeting, make notes regarding **After the** attendance and any special things that have been learnt **"At Home"** about those who attended.

These notes can be made on one of the lists of names supplied by the Organising Committee.

16   Celling Youth
(Small Groups in Youth Ministry)

The use of small groups in youth ministry is quite a new concept in the local church situation. Perhaps because we are more content with the familiar, and acceptable style of youth programme, the venture to something new is risky. Few want to risk altering the 'tried-for-years', on-going, semi-satisfactory, perhaps unchallenging youth programme for something new and different. This chapter will outline some models which will serve to show how varied small group ministry can be.

Reasons to contemplate using small groups

In a large youth group these problems could exist:
— lack of personal contact with each other
— lack of personal contact with leaders
— shy people who find it hard to contribute, especially in large groups
— easier to avoid getting involved in a large group
— difficult to maintain effective control

The list could go on, but small group techniques can overcome these problems, and result in a more effective youth ministry.

In his book *The People Dynamic,* Howard Clinebell Jr. suggests that "no age group is more concerned than youth about finding and fulfilling themselves. No age segment of a community can use growth groups more productively."

Liverpool youth cells

I pioneered one of the early Youth Cell experiments in New South Wales in the Liverpool Uniting Parish in 1969. The population of the area served by the Liverpool Circuit at that time was 80,000, having rapidly increased to that figure due to the Green Valley Housing Commission area. There were existing youth programmes in the circuit, but because of diversity of backgrounds, age ranges and Christian growth some groups were having problems with control. Many young people were virtually left to "bring themselves up", and therefore many appreciated the chance to just talk with an adult who was interested in them.

With these factors in mind, a meeting was called, and a Youth Cell Programme was implemented, using an adaptation of a plan first developed by Henry A. Tani, Youth Director of the United Church of Christ (Evangelical and Reformed Congregational Churches — U.S.A.) The plan is outlined in his book *Ventures in Youth Work,* (Christian Education Press, U.S.) I had also experimented in youth cell work at Wesley Church, Hamilton, and had observed a similar experiment in an Episcopal Church in Montclaire, New Jersey (N.Y.).

1. Small groups of approximately 8-12 persons meet in **The plan** the homes of group members preferably each week. **in brief**
2. The programme is intended for young people of high school age and over.
3. Groups meet for set periods with a minimum length of three months.
4. Adult Counsellors are assigned to each group to share in the activity in their role as "enablers"; they are the key to the success of the programme.
5. Combined activities are held for all groups including those who don't participate in the youth cells.
6. Basic requirements are—
   (a) Regular attendance of group meetings and full participation and acceptance of responsibility by each member.
   (b) Specific goals are pursued with full emphasis given to service and study aspects.
7. Flexibility. The plan allows for the initiative of counsellors and group members. Experimentation within the broad principles governing this activity is encouraged.
8. To ensure adequate evaluation and development, the whole scheme is controlled by a representative body.

1. *Names and groupings of potential cell members.* Lists **The structure** were made of all young people in existing youth groups, **of Liverpool** together with age and address. These were then divided **cell groups** into groups based upon age, locality and mutual interest — they comprised both sexes. Attention was given to the

"actives" and "inactives" in order to create a healthy balance.

2. *Counsellors.* Counsellors were assigned to each group. These became leaders in most cases because of the inexperience and lack of initiative of cell members. From our 12 cell groups, half were led by married couples and others by two of the senior young people — preferably "a male and a female".

3. *Location.* The ideal was for each group to meet in the home of one of its members (including that of the Counsellors, if available) rotating to a different house each week. This, in a natural fashion, exposes the young people to the parents of those homes, which is an important aspect of the total group experience.

4. *Group Leaders.* In each group one of the young people was to be elected leader or rostered leaders made for each night. Two representatives were to be made to the Youth Council and a treasurer for the group.

5. *Finance.* Each student member was to pay 10 cents a night, "workers" 20 cents. 20 per cent of the funds to go to the Youth Council.

6. *Frequency.* Each group met once a week on Friday night for a term of approximately 3 months. After 2-3 weeks break, the group resumed.

7. *Goals.* Ideally each group was to seek to achieve the four goals listed below. In particular, those of study and service were seen to be the backbone of the programme.

   (a) *Study Goal.* To undertake a major study in an area of mutual interest. This was determined by the use of "interest indicator" sheets and a group decision based on the findings from these sheets. A number of other methods were also used to reach a group decision.

   (b) *Service Goal.* To undertake one service project — to be decided upon by each group. Suggestions were made to those groups who had no ideas.

   (c) *Skill Goal.* To learn at least one new skill — the group to determine a skill in which they wish to become proficient. Skills were not solely manual but embracing development in understanding and relating to people and society as a whole.

(d) *Social Goal.* To plan and hold social events for the group, and on occasion for the combined cells.

8. *Combined Activities.* Also as part of the Youth Cell programme combined activities were planned to prevent isolation of small groups and to offer an opportunity for fellowship for those Church young people who may not be involved in the small group plan. Other activities for "outreach" were also included.

9. *Youth Council.* The above activities were the responsibility of the Parish Youth Council, membership of which was made up of the Counsellors and two representatives from each group. This met bi-monthly.

10. *Youth Cell Counsellors Meeting.* It was also part of the programme that all Youth Cell Counsellors met bi-monthly where membership, follow-up programmes, problems, etc., were discussed.

11. *Control and Organisation.* The total programme was under the direct supervision of the Minister and Deaconess and the control of the Parish Youth Council.

12. *Training and Evaluation.* At the end of each year a leader's training and evaluation weekend is held.

13. *Manual.* A prepared manual was given to each Counsellor, which set out the background and principles of the Youth Cell method, together with suggestions and resources for Bible Study, Service and Skill, Goals, etc. An outline of the Goals and Counsellor's role, and methods of Bible Study were also included.

14. *Commencement.* A special orientation night was planned for the commencement of each cell. Counsellors personally visited all those on their list, inviting them to a "Special" evening. This night was planned to be rather informal with plenty of games, and an extra special supper.
Following this, the plan and whole procedure was outlined to the young people using flip charts and then a duplicated sheet spelling out and illustrating basic ideas of the youth cells was given to each one so that they could show it to their parents.

Plan in detail

1. Small groups

(i) Composition

(a) The active members of the Church-oriented youth are divided into units of approximately 8 to 12 persons. The division is based upon age, geography and mutual interest. As far as possible there is not a large spread of ages in any one group. Various age groupings are formed into separate groups, e.g. extremes such as 13 years and 20 years are avoided.

While age, to a large extent, determines mutual interest, those with specific interests are grouped together, e.g. those undertaking higher education (University or Teachers College).

In a parish where the youth membership is drawn from a wide area, those from a given section would possibly be assigned to one group. This is necessary in the case of younger groups who do not have their own transport. Each group is made up of both boys and girls.

(b) To each small group is assigned two inactive young people who are only on the fringe of the Church young programme. It is the responsibility of the small group to seek to involve these two persons in their group life. As soon as the inactive ones have become active, two more inactive ones are assigned.

This saves the cell from becoming a clique and keeps constantly before it the necessity to reach out to others, thus preventing self-centredness and bringing new life into the group.

(c) Counsellors are assigned to each group. They are the key to the success of the programme. Married couples are the ideal. The counsellors share in all the meetings and other activities of the group. They are committed to serve only for the period of the small group's existence. They are responsible to and helped by the Co-ordinator who supervises this youth programme.

(ii) Location

Each group meets in the homes of its members (including that of the counsellors, if available), rotating to a different home each week. This provides a close informal atmosphere and, in a natural fashion, exposes the youth people and counsellors to the parents in those homes. This is an important aspect of the total group existence and provides important communication between the counsellor and parents.

(iii) Frequency

Each group determines the frequency and time of their own meetings. Ideally each group should meet once a week (or at least once every two weeks). Some groups have met on week nights, Sunday afternoons, at 7 p.m. on Sunday evenings (a junior group) or after evening church service.

(iv) Duration

Groups meet for terms — the minimum being three months. This stated period of time will be determined by the interests and commitments of each group, e.g. those still pursuing a course of study may want to avoid examination periods.

(v) Regular Meeting Procedure

(a) *Leadership.* Generally the member of the group in whose home the meeting is held chairs that meeting. This may not involve a great deal of work but it is important that each person be given the opportunity to develop leadership potential.

The study session may or may not be led by the person in the chair. However, generally the person chairing the evening links the evening's study to the previous meeting by giving a prepared summary of the main points of the past study. This may also be done with other sections of the meeting.

The Chair-person also acts as time-keeper, introduces and thanks the guest speakers etc. and ensures that visitors are welcomed.

The adult counsellors act only in an advisory capacity. Their role is to act as resource persons, guide the group in making its decisions, generally supervise the conduct of the group and do other such things as may help promote the effectiveness of the group. The degree of involvement by the counsellors is determined by the age of the cell.

(b) *Length of Meeting.* This is determined ahead of time and strictly adhered to. An hour and a half has been found to be sufficient for most groups. Meetings should begin on time and end on time.

(c) *Content of Meetings.* This depends on the exact nature of the goals each group selects. Past experiments suggest that the first 40 to 50 minutes should be spent on the study topic and discussion with the balance of the time devoted to skill training or planning for the group service project, etc., and ending with supper.

(vi) Goals

During its life each group seeks to do four things. A group may find that several meetings are required to survey the possibilities before they agree on their choice.

Ideally each group should seek to achieve the four goals listed below. Although this may not be possible for various reasons, it is essential that the service and study goals represent the "backbone" of the programme.

(a) *Study Goal*

To undertake a major study of an area of mutual interest. This may be determined by the use of "interest indicator" sheets and a group decision based on the findings from these sheets. A variety of study resources will need to be made available to the groups in order that the chosen course of study can be followed. Previous experiments have had a library or resources from which counsellors could draw.

(b) *Service Goal*

To undertake one service project during the group's existence. Again, this is decided upon by each group. A list of suggested projects should be supplied to each counsellor. These may be used if the group does not have any ideas regarding specific tasks. In some cases other groups may be invited by a group to join them. Frequently the study goal may suggest areas of need.

(c) *Skill Goal*

To learn at least one new skill.

The group will determine a skill in which they wish to become proficient. A list of suggestions which should be supplied to the counsellors may help a decision to be reached. Included in some previous lists have been operation of movie projectors, chairmanship of meetings, recreational leadership, first aid, boy-girl relationships, current economic and political issues on a national or international level, world understanding (study of other countries), voice production, drama.

One or two members may have a flair for one activity which they will introduce to the group. The group might make itself proficient in a certain field and then share this interest with the total youth fellowship group at combined meetings or conduct a skill session for a single cell.

(d) *Social Goal*

To plan and hold social events for the group. This may expand to the preparation of a programme for the combined groups. The counsellor is involved in all social events.

2. Combined Activities

The aim of these is to prevent isolation of small groups by providing a rallying point for all.

They offer an opportunity for fellowship for those Church young people who may not be involved in the small groups.

These have included a wide variety of activities in previous experiments. The following are a selection of some events.

Youth Services

Both individuals and groups participate in organising and conducting these services. Some groups have been involved in extensive planning of creative worship services. One group climaxed weeks of studying the purpose of worship with a weekend retreat to plan a most creative worship service.

Youth teas

The programme for the teas is arranged by one of the group on a group basis, with the Youth Teas Sub-Committee of the Parish Youth Council being consulted. Such matters as, publicity and variety in the programme are the responsibility of the rostered group. Also, the leadership of the tea is in the hands of a group member (not a counsellor). The rostered group is also encouraged to invite one or more other church or non-church groups to the tea.

Camps

The youth cells are involved in planning for parish youth camps, with cells given particular responsibilities. Some groups have organised their own weekend house party, sometimes inviting a few of their own age group who are not involved in the group.

Social activities

As the programme develops, groups are assigned the responsibility of planning monthly social activities for the combined groups and other Church youth. In the early stages specific groups may offer to arange these at irregular intervals. Previous programmes have included:— hikes, harbour cruises, beach parties, bus trips, coffee hours and a variety of evening social events.

3. The Counsellors

The key to success of this small group plan is the counsellor or advisor. They do not need to be "experts", but need to be sympathetic to young people and able to accept an advisory rather than a leadership role. At the same time they uphold certain standards of behaviour and group discipline and entering into meaningful dialogue with them.

Availability outside the group situations will be necessary as they gain the confidence of young people. As already indicated, each group is assigned counsellors, in most cases married couples. They will be involved in all activities of the group for its term of existence.

Every assistance will be given to them by the Co-ordinator, who will conduct training sessions for counsellors prior to the inauguration of the plan.

Regular meetings of counsellors are held. This gives support to the counsellors and provides opportunity for co-ordination, evaluation and planning.

Leadership study resources and other materials to assist counsellors fulfil their roles within the group should be supplied.

4. Control and organisation

The total programme should be under the control of a Parish Youth Council which should include all adult counsellors and two members of each cell (as well as representatives of other youth movements in the Parish).

Evaluation

Regular evaluations of the Liverpool Programme were held. In November 1971, three years after the commencement of the Youth Cell Programme, an evaluation was carried out at two levels, one by a combined senior group, and the other at a Leaders' Conference.

Following a discussion regarding the aims of youth work the advantages and disadvantages of cells were considered against large groups.

Advantages of small groups
— More individual attention
— Get to know each other better
— Everyone participates and contributes in discussion (helps shy ones)
— Better control is possible
— Study preparation and presentation easier, especially when group members lead.

Disadvantages of small groups
— Some homes limit active games
— People can't drift in
— Numbers are limited
— If members lose programme, different venues can be a hindrance
— Don't get to know other age groups.

Advantages of large groups
— Easy not to get involved
— People can drift in (can be *disadvantage,* too!)
— Fewer leaders needed
— Meet our friends as a whole
— Depends on young people — whether co-operative or "knockers"
— Group grows more easily.

Disadvantages of large groups
— Impersonal — don't get to know others at depth
— Special accommodation needed
— Hard to maintain control
— Lack of concentration
— Difficult to cater for all interests
— Wide range of age group more difficult.

Without knowing what evaluation the young people themselves had done, the leaders were asked to list the advantages and disadvantages also. It is interesting to note similar points brought out.

Advantages of small groups
- Studies can be geared to specific age-group levels
- More personal contact with the individual at greater depth
- Individual concern improves because:—
  - Members get to know leader better
  - Groups get to know each other better and develops concern
  - Contact with home of members
  - Contact with home of leaders
- Better learning situation
- Less discipline problem
- Greater sense of belonging (e.g. this is my group)
- Evaluation easier with small group, e.g. successes and failures.

Disadvantages of small groups
- Problems of isolation — can develop into a "clique"
- Within the closeness of this cell relationship, young people become aware of the leader's weaknesses (as well as strengths)
- The limits to leader's availability to the individual in the group
- The physical and emotional limitations of the leader at the end of a busy week
- Bigger burden upon the leader—
  - because totally responsible for whole programme and behaviour of cell (in large group, usually others — committee, etc. share this responsibility)
  - need for leaders to have only one task to fulfil in local church
- Small disadvantage in not belonging to state-wide youth body — cell not easily identified when talking with outsiders.
- Larger number of leaders required
- Small groups don't allow for a big fall-off — when group too small doesn't operate effectively. Also, small groups don't allow for much increase — a group that becomes too large becomes ineffective
- To divide a group that becomes too large can lead to a fall-off of weaker members. Suggestion: When a group becomes too big work as two groups in one larger home and slowly divide into separate activities

— Lack of available homes within the group, especially so in this experiment due to reasons given earlier.

In an evaluation some four and a half years after the **A further** Youth Cells commenced at Liverpool, Richard Kirby drew **evaluation** attention to such points as:

(a) A comprehensive training course was needed for counsellors to learn to lead a cell properly.
(b) Regular attendance by cell members should be a concentrated aim.
(c) problems seemed to be:
    (i)   Limited access to homes
    (ii) Suitable study material
    (iii) Suitable service projects.

These recommendations were made by Richard Kirby
(1) Do not lead a group on your own.
(2) Counsellors not to take an active leadership role.
(3) Need for counsellors to be available outside group situation for approach by younger people or their parents.

In conclusion, he comments "Cells came to run and govern themselves. The Cell programme has been extremely successful: If you are having a problem in your youth group due to size or lack of personal contact then the cell programme has a great deal left to offer you".

The Reverend Don Drury, who succeeded me as Super- **An up to date** intendent Minister, made these comments seven years after **evaluation** the formation of the first youth cells.

"The Cell approach to youth work basically has proved to be an effective one. Our cells range in size from eight to fifteen and continue to meet in the homes of cell members. Cells are grouped according to age. Young people clearly appreciate the security and significance of belonging to a cell 'family' providing it is functioning healthily.

Effective functioning of a cell is very much dependent on suitable leadership—

• Young people and adults who are alive to God through their Saviour, Jesus Christ, and who function in the power of the Holy Spirit.
• They will function with gifts and ministries given them by the Lord.

- They will develop a sensiivity and understanding of the young people in the Lord.
- They will learn to exercise authority in the Lord.
- Their central task will be to help their cell members to come alive to God in Jesus Christ, and to learn to function in the power of the Holy Spirit.
- They will develop a balanced cell programme — worship and study the Word of God at the centre, with a healthy flow on of social, recreational and service activities.
- They will train cell members to be responsible for as many of these activities as possible.

It is most helpful to have a team of two or three leaders on each cell with a variety of gifts and ministries. This is also helpful for musical talent, cars for transport, as well as providing support for leaders. Have additional supportive leadership. For example, have the ministers or other suitable people come in and contribute to the cell from time to time. Or take the cell group to particularly strong, supportive homes from time to time.

Leaders need proper maintenance and encouragement. It is important to meet for fellowship, prayer and training. Switch leadership around when not 'jelling' properly. A group may lack motivation, healthy creative growth, and spiritual impact if leadership doesn't click.

Relationship to whole Church

Avoid having a cell group become too self-centred or isolationist by creating a proper relationship to the rest of the Church family. There must be combined cell activities from time to time, e.g. combined junior camps and combined senior cells. Also combined junior youth camps and combined senior youth camps prove tremendous growth points. These need to be open to all parish young people as some young people don't belong to cell groups.

It is important that the whole Church family be one in Christ or else the uniting, reconciling power of the Gospel is not being fully realized. Some ways we have seen this working out include vital worship, regular Parish Teas for all ages, sharing together on activities such as a Parish Fair, learning together in a Parish Family Camp and participation in the Sunday Christian Education Programme. It is valuable, too, to have the whole Church interested in the youth cell programme, and, above all, to have its constant prayerful support".

It is important to stress that the Liverpool Youth Cell **Other models**
Programme was but one approach to small group ministry,
and many other churches are using small group concepts
in many and various ways to bring young people to a
closer relationship with Jesus Christ our Saviour and Lord.

In the Pittwater Regional Mission, the old and the new **Pittwater**
have been combined by maintaining the Friday night youth **Regional Mission**
group, but using small group principles to facilitate a more
worthwhile programme.

Cliff Powell and David Freeston made these comments
when evaluating their small group programme.

"In the middle of 1974 the Young Leaders' Fellowship
of the Pittwater Regional Mission made the transition from
a large group youth work to a small groups programme.
Up until that time the group, averaging 70 to 80 young
people of High School age and above (including 15-20
leaders), had run about as well as could be expected.
Leader/group member relations were good, discipline was
satisfactory, and a good proportion of the Friday nights
seemed worthwhile in terms of the material presented, the
level of group interest, etc. It was, then, with no pressing
sense of dissatisfaction, but rather an undefined feeling
that perhaps we could do better, that a group of 12 leaders
began attending the Basic Small Groups Training Course
to see what it could offer us for our youth work. It wasn't
long before we were convinced of the value of a change-
over to a small groups programme."

The primary aim set by the Pittwater Regional Mission
was outreach, "To present the Gospel in terms relevant to
our young people".

The weekly routine for leaders and group members.

(a) Leaders' evaluation and Preparation Session. The
meeting was basically to evaluate the previous week's
programme, discuss problems, prepare for future evenings,
and share in prayer. This meeting has become a vital part
of the programme, as the leaders' group has in itself
become a real koinonia group, blending members into a
real leadership team.

(b) Friday night meeting: All members meet at the
Church buildings at 8.00 p.m. until 10.00 p.m. where, after

five to fifteen minutes of announcements, the members break into small groups and the groups meet for about an hour. Each group comprising a leader, an assistant leader, and six to ten young yeople. To finish the night off, all members re-assemble after group time and a games programme is held until 10.00 p.m.

One problem area was inconsistent attendance by some members in each group, therefore preventing establishment of group cohesion. To overcome this problem a brief explanation was made to the whole group about the advantages of consistent attendance, stressing that it enabled the leader and group to get to know and trust each other. We also discussed the potential of a group who were able to be honest with each other about hang-ups, doubts, questions, experiences, etc. Following this, the young people were asked to "Contract" to attend at least five out of the following six weeks, and thus the formation of consistent and inconsistent groups has been tried, but not evaluated as this was written.

A regular annual four day camp in August/September is an important part of the Pittwater programme, and their leaders see the importance of the camp in this way.

"In some respects, what we have begun to build in our Friday night groups, has found its fullest fruition in such a camp."

Special commitment nights were held, to afford young people, who were feeling the need for deeper commitment the opportunity to seek special counselling with leaders but it was discontinued due to the break in continuity of the normal Small Group Programme.

Some of the insights gained by the Pittwater team could be listed in this way.

1. The need to be well organised, and have trained leaders working as a team.
2. Simple rules to govern the programme.
3. A willingness to experiment with new ideas.
4. A specially designed study programme, to suit specific needs of the groups.
5. An effort to keep parents in contact with the programme, by constant letters, and personal contact where possible.
6. Programme well prepared and circulated to all group members, showing variety and encouraging regular attendance.

The Punchbowl/Greenacre Uniting Parish has organised a Youth Cell Programme which is quite similar in structure to the Liverpool experiment. **Punchbowl/ Greenacre Youth Cells**

The programme is organised by a director, Mr. Bruce Rickard, and below you see part of a circular which he uses to publicize the cell groups and gives insights to the organisation of the groups.

"The 'Cell Groups' is the name given to the Youth Organisation which caters for the range of High School students and young workers. The purpose of this organization is to provide a fellowship of fun and learning, to encourage young people into a personal relationship with Christ as their Saviour and Lord.

The 'Four-Square' programme covers physical, social, mental and spiritual aspects of life. Each night these aspects are included and each individual is expected to participate in games and discussion to the best of their ability. Privileges and responsibilities go hand in hand and so to enjoy the one you will be expected to gradually share the other.

This year a five-week-cycle is being followed; three weeks in homes for regular cell meetings, followed by one week combined (with various activities being available simultaneously for various groups or individuals in turn) and the next weekend an outing for all groups, sometimes all to the one place but at other times all separately or in various combinations of groups as desired. That same weekend there will be held a Fellowship Tea where everyone brings tucker to share and a varied programme follows. Occasionally we may have a guest speaker or a film etc.

To streamline finances members pay 50c. (school children) or $1.00 (workers) in a lump sum at the first cell meeting in the home. This covers the five weeks. Anyone missing a meeting will be expected to contribute the same amount as we are planning to buy equipment of various kinds, e.g. for games and lighting, and to further improve facilities.

Leaders of groups will be varied each term and regular attendance is expected from all. A few groups suffered from individuals "swapping" groups without permission and these people must realise that this affects smoothness of operation to the extent that it cannot be allowed.

You must be willing to co-operate and play your part

to further improve this activity which is designed for your enjoyment and benefit."

Some special features of the cell programme at this church would seem to be:

(a) A "Spin-In" night. An evening of groups coming together, and each member bringing a friend is a good way of advertising. A note of warning is added — it needs to be well planned.

(b) As part of the programme, but run by a separate committee, the "Coffee Shop" is held monthly after the 'monthly guest service'. The committee assist on special nights as required.

(c) Camping is a highlight in this programme; the level of participation is very high, and well planned programmes have made this activity a very useful instrument in the youth programme.

(d) The commitment to an effective service programme is in the form of some annual events. An "Aged Citizens' Dinner" near Easter, a "Walk against Want", organization of the "Smith Family Food Drive" in their area and participation in various doorknock appeals.

(e) Some of the cell groups have organized religious musicals with great success. "Jubilation" and "I'm here, God's here, Now we can start" have been an important cell group activity.

Bruce Rickard suggests these points as words of warning and some helpful suggestions to other groups.

1. Enlistment of younger members of the church as assistant counsellors and counsellors-in-training can be useful but under no circumstances can you do without a sprinkling of solid, dedicated, lively but capable older-type counsellors who can apply firmness when required.

2. Leadership problems should be attacked in two ways. Firstly, a complete training programme so that people will feel confident to take up positions as counsellors. And secondly, to have 'Reserve Counsellors' fully trained, who can and do take over on occasions when, through illness, holidays or other reasons, the original counsellors cannot attend their groups.

3. All young people themelves should be actively involved right throughout the programme from planning to execution.

4. Cell Group Counsellor meetings are of great importance and attendance is essential, and therefore it is important that a director of youth cells ensures that these meetings are vital in content and operation.

The Dodecs

This is the name given to the Small Group plan structured by the Department of Christian Education in Adelaide. This plan you will see is quite different to the Liverpool experiment, insofar as it strives for a twelve month covenant by ten young people and two enablers.

Here are their aims:

(1) To enable youth, for whom the Christian faith has begun to have meaning, to meet together for study, reflection, and thus Christian growth.
(2) To so strengthen the core group members; that they will gain an increasing concern for others.
(3) To establish and strengthen the links between youth and "significant" adults in the Church.
(4) To enable youth to develop deeper relationships with each other and aid the establishment of personal identity.
(5) To develop the discipline of loyalty and group responsibility by means of a covenant and establish the need for commitment.
(6) To develop leadership qualities by a pattern of involvement and decision making and programming.
(7) To discover the promises of the gospel within a small group experience.
(8) To enable the increasing exercise of responsible action in the community.

Dodec means twelve. A Dodec group usually consists of twelve people, 10 youth and two adult (enablers). Such a group can fit into two cars which can be used to gather up the group, or to give it mobility when necessary. The minimum number in a group should not be less than ten (including the enablers). If a group is as large as 18, then two more enablers should be found and two Dodec groups formed. The 12 is maintained in the following way:

(i) by covenanting with each other to stay together for one year and by developing a "community of caring" where each accepts responsibilities for each other;
(ii) by a member withdrawing only if he can be replaced. If a member must withdraw, the group must immediately replace him. Thus individual members are now their own recruiters.

The Covenant

A Dodec group is formed when a number are prepared to enter into a covenant with each other

A member of a Dodec group undertakes:

(1) to be a responsible group member, honest, with the others, accepting responsibility to them, and to be a regular attender for the extent of the group's life. (This would normally be a twelve month period).

(2) to undertake a searching discussion or study on topics of interest selected by the group and make a sincere and open search for faith

(3) to share in the leadership, planning and activities of the group

(4) to be involved in the Church's life through worship, and in some project of social help and outreach.

Age: The plan is for fourth year high school or 16 years of age and over. The plan suggests that the group should meet at least once a fortnight, for two hours, and this could include a meal.

At least one service project to be undertaken each year, to involve:

— research into a community need

— two-by-two contact with persons involved in the problem

— provisions of some material assistance.

Exchange twice yearly with other Dodec groups, so that ideas can be exchanged.

To avoid the danger of cliques, the group undertakes to be involved in a larger group, to actively engage in sponsorship of other youth activity and worship services.

The Enabler

"The Dodecs" require two enablers to be associated with the group. Generally the group will have a part in the selection of the enablers. The adults have been called Enablers because that name seems more in line with their role than, for instance, Adult Counsellor or Leader.

Ross Snyder speaks of an Enabler (though he calls him or her an "Adult Guarantor") as a "significant other" who is farther along in life. The enablers would "not do for the group what it is able to do for itself". They are encouraged to fulfil basic training requirements, e.g. Group Life Laboratory and attend a study/training "Meal for Enablers" regularly.

SENIOR YOUTH CELL PROGRAM

LIVERPOOL METHODIST   MAY – AUGUST

DATE	LOCATION	STUDY TOPIC	STUDY LEADER	SKILL TOPIC	SKILL LEADER	OUTING	SUPPER DUTY
MAY 7th	TWEEDS	MAJOR WORLD RELIGIONS ① JUDAISM	J. MALLISON	TAKING GOOD PHOTOS – AND DEVELOPING AND PRINTING	J. MALLISON		ALBIE CHRIS FRANCES
14th	PARSONAGE	WHAT IS A MISSIONARY?	A. BRADLEY MISSIONARY BUILDER	SLIDES – AUSTRALIAN ABORIGINES IN ARNHEM LAND	A. BRADLEY		DAVID KAY
21st	FOWLERS	MAJOR WORLD RELIGIONS ② ISLAM	BRENDA MAUREEN SANDA	HOW TO SPIN YOUR MONEY OUT – BUDGETING FOR TEENS	W. DOUST J. MALLISON		LYN CHRIS RANDA
28th	CIRCUIT CAMP AT OTFORD						
JUNE 4th	TWEEDS	MAJOR WORLD RELIGIONS ③ HINDUISM	LYN CLIVE KAY	HOW TO FLY – PART ① – LECTURE + FILM	J.D. SIM FLYING OFFICER R.A.A.F. RESERVE		FRANCES KAY CHRIS
11th	HILLVIEW HALL	MAJOR WORLD RELIGIONS ④ BUDDHISM	NARRELLE WAYNE ALBIE	CARPENTRY + CRAFT NIGHT – MAKING DAYLIGHT SCREENS FOR S.S.	A. FRAGAR CARPENTER + TECH. LECTURER		BRENDA LINDA CAROLYN
18th	FOWLERS	SELF UNDERSTANDING ① WHO AM I? ② WHAT AM I HERE FOR?	J. MALLISON	INSPECTION AMBULANCE STATION – LECTURE/DEMO ARTIFICIAL RESPIRATION	MR. SWEEHAN MR. KNOWLES		MAUREEN LYN
25th	TWEEDS	SELF UNDERSTANDING ② HOW TO FIND PURPOSE IN LIFE	FRANCES LINDA CHRIS	WHAT MAKES A CAR "TICK" – LECTURE/FILM INTERNAL COMB. ENGINE	R. KIRBY of B.M.C.		DAVID JILL CAMPBELL
JULY 2nd						TEN PIN BOWLING	
9th	PARSONAGE	SELF UNDERSTANDING ④ HANDLING OUR HANGUPS	J. MALLISON	HOW TO FLY – PART ② – LECTURE + FILM	J.D. SIM R.A.A.F. RES.		ALBIE CHRIS FRANCES
16th	WALLIS'	SELF UNDERSTANDING ③ RELATING TO OTHERS	DAVID LYN CLIVE	MYSTERY NIGHT	MR. + MRS. D. WALLIS		DAVID KAY
23rd	TWEEDS	COMMUNICATING WITH GOD ① WHAT IS PRAYER?	FRANCES CAROLYN	DOING THE RIGHT THING! – LECTURE/DEMO ETIQUETTE FOR TEENS	MRS. J. TWEED		CLIVE NARELLE
30th	COMBINED CELLS NIGHT						
AUG. 6th	HILLVIEW HALL	COMMUNICATING WITH GOD ② BUGS IN THE SYSTEM	LINDA CHRIS RANDA	CARPENTRY + CRAFT NIGHT	A. FRAGAR		WAYNE JILL CAROLYN
13th	TWEEDS	COMMUNICATING WITH GOD ③ THE PERFECT PRAYER	DAVID LYN	FIRST AID FOR THE INJURED – LECTURE + PRACTICAL SESSION	E. GRAHAM 1st AID OFFICER		LYN CHRIS RANDA
20th	FOWLERS	COMMUNICATING WITH GOD ④ TAKING GOD UP ON HIS WORD	BRENDA LINDA DAVID	THE EMERGING NATION TO OUR NORTH (SLIDES ON PAPUA)	MATRON MCRAE		MAUREEN DAVID MAY
27th						ICE SKATING (ASSEMBLE AT LIB.)	

GROUP COUNSELLOR: REV. J. MALLISON
TREASURERS: KAY AND FRANCES
SECRETARIES: KRISTINE AND BRENDA
YOUTH COUNCIL REPS: KRISTINE, WAYNE, CLIVE, MAUREEN

ADDRESSES OF MEETING PLACES:
FOWLERS: 68 RESERVOIR RD, KINGSGROVE
TWEEDS: 285 STONEY CREEK RD, HECKENBURG
WALLIS: 45 GUTHEGA CRES, MT PRITCHARD
HILLVIEW HALL: HUE RD, HILLVIEW

WEEKLY FEE: 20¢ 'WORKERS', 10¢ STUDENTS

STUDY BOOKS:
* "SO WHAT'S THE DIFFERENCE"
* "TEACH US TO PRAY"
* STUDY NOTES ON PRAYER

STARTING TIME: 7.45 P.M.

IF YOU CAN'T KEEP YOUR ABOVE COMMITMENT ...... ARRANGE FOR SOMEONE ELSE TO TAKE YOUR PLACE – DON'T LET THE GROUP DOWN!

SUPPER: BOYS AS WELL AS GIRLS RESPONSIBLE FOR FOOD AND WASHING-UP

TRANSPORT: ALL PASSENGERS CONTRIBUTE TO DRIVER'S

17 Resources for Small Groups

This section is designed to help the group and group leader appreciate the resources that are available to them as they plan a programme or work out the syllabus for a group.

If there is a multi-cell programme, that is more than one group operating at the one time, there is value in the leaders or group representatives getting together and finding out what the needs of the people are and what topics they want to study. A course can then be worked out that could allow a common theme to be studied.

If it is decided to use expensive resources such as a film or hired cassette material the group members might decide to put aside a small amount of money each week towards the hire costs. A film showing could also be a time to make an effort to interest other people in the small group concept. It could also be the occasion for the combining of one or more groups for an evening.

Another very good reason for having good and adequate resources is the problem of shared ignorance in the group. This is not meant to denigrate the group members, but on occasion groups have encountered problems because there was no one with sufficient authority or knowledge to either help the group or to act as a check to the group. When it is considered that some group study methods require depth preparation then it can be seen that the more knowledge available to the group then the more creative will be the group experience. Again Bible study methods suggest bringing in an 'expert' after the group has done its work using the Inductive Method. If the group cannot get a person as the expert, then there is no better resource than some of the excellent one-volume Bible commentaries that are available.

Perhaps a member of a small group or groups could act as librarian and assist the sharing of books among members of the group.

Check, too, what is available from your local municipal libraries — nct just for books on religion, but on sociology, group theory and dynamics, craft ideas, camping and bush-walking.

This list is not exhaustive. You can fill in the gaps by browsing through the appropriate sections in Christian and other bookshops.

BIBLE BACKGROUND

David and Pat Alexander (ed.), *The Lion Handbook to the Bible* (Anzea, 1973) — a very useful resource book — pictures, maps, charts, expert articles, concordance and commentaries.

G. W. Anderson, *A Critical Introduction to the Old Testament* (Duckworth, 1960).

G. W. Anderson, *The History and Religion in Israel* (O.U.P., 1966) in *New Clarendon Bible.* The other books in this series are well worth owning.

William Barclay, *Introducing the Bible* (The Bible Reading Fellowship The International Bible Reading Association, 1972) — Dr. Barclay testifies to the value of the Bible as an inspired and unique book and gives clear advice on how best to read it and how the biblical writings came into being and finally gained acceptance as Scripture. Most important of all, he presents the Bible as a book to be read and enjoyed today.

J. D. Douglas (ed.), *New Bible Dictionary* (1960).

H. L. Ellison, *Men Spake from God* (The Prophets), (Paternoster Press, 1958).

D. Guthrie, *New Testament Introduction* (I.V.P., 1971).

John L. McKenzie, *Dictionary of the Bible* (Geoffrey Chapman, 1965).

William Neil, *The Bible Story* (Joint Board of Christian Education).

William Neil, *The Importance of the Bible* (Joint Board of Christian Education, 1975).

Eric Osborn, *The Bible: The Word in the World* (Joint Board of Christian Education, 1969 — Christian Life Basic Book).

BIBLE COMMENTARIES

One Volume

The Interpreters Bible Commentary (Collins).

The Jerome Biblical Commentary, ed. R. E. Brown, J. A. Fitzmyer and R. E. Murray (Geoffrey Chapman, 1970).

The New Bible Commentary Revised, ed. D. Guthrie and J. A. Motyer (3rd edition, Inter-Varsity Press, 1970).

William Neil, *One Volume Commentary* (Hodder and Stoughton, 1962). (Available as a paperback).

M. Black and H. H. Rowley (ed.) *Peake's Commentary* (Nelson, 1962). (F. F. Bruce, a noted conservative scholar is one of the contributors. The only thing the same as the old *Peake* is the name.)

John R. W. Stott, *Understanding the Bible* (Anzea, 1972).

Robert C. Walton (ed.), *A Source Book of the Bible for Teachers* (SCM, 1970).

Single Book Commentaries

William Barclay, *Daily Study Bible* (St. Andrews Press, Edinburgh). Whole of New Testament.

Pelican *Commentaries;* Most of the New Testament; somewhat scholarly for most general readers.

S.C.M. *Torch* Series — covers whole of Bible.

Scripture Union *Bible Study* books, *Bible Characters* and *Bible Doctrines.* Can be used for daily reading or as a source book for group work. Written by leading Bible teachers and scholars. *Daily Bread,* a daily reading book, also contains a supplement for Group Bible Study.

R. V. Tasker (ed.), *The Tyndale New Testament Commentaries* (Tyndale, London).

BIBLE STUDY

The Bethel Series (Adult Education Foundation, Madison, Wisc.).

Christian Life Curriculum, *Books of the Bible Series; Themes in John; Acts: The Community of Faith; Psalms of Faith and Hope; Isaiah: The Vision of Service; On the Mount; Jonah; Moses (Studies in Exodus); Faith and Freedom (Galatians); A Matter of Life and Death (1 John)* — Published by The Joint Board of Christian Education. — A series of short studies on a specific theme. Highly recommended.

Christians Under Construction — a cassette set of studies in *Ephesians* with Discussion Guide. An in-depth 12 session study from the Institute of Lay Renewal. 1610 La Vista Road, Northeast Atlanta, Georgia, 30329. USA.

Derek B. Copley, *Home Bible Studies* (Paternoster Press, 1972). The sub-title of this book is Forming and Running an Adult Group. Mr. Copley is a Bible College Principal and has had practical experience in group life and work.

Joy Davidman, *Smoke on the Mountain* — on the ten commandments.

Christian Outreach, *Growth by Groups* (Christian Outreach — Box 115 Huntingdon Valley, Penna, 19006. U.S.A.) — A resource book in itself with a number of studies that get to grips with direct Bible work. Suitable for adult groups and recommended.

J. Hills Cotterill and Michael Hews, *Know How to Lead Bible Study and Discussion Groups* — a booklet in the Know How series (Scripture Union, London, 1963).

John Frederick Jansen, *Exercises in Interpreting Scripture* (Geneva Press, 1968). This book seeks to assist the layman in developing his own skills of interpretation. It is a readable and an inspiring treatment.

Donald E. Miller, Graydon F. Snyder, Robert W. Neff, *Using Biblical Simulations* (Judson Press, 1973) — Can be used in group work, in worship services. A Biblical Simulation is the re-enactment of some particular Biblical event in an attempt to portray accurately some selected features of that event.

Karl A. Olsson, *Find Yourself in the Bible* (Augsburg Publishing House, Minneapolis, Minnesota, 1974) — A Guide to Relational Bible Study for Small Groups. Olsson leads the reader to identify with the warm and compelling action of real people. He shares the excitement he felt in discovering the Bible's personal meaning for his own life.

Roy H. Ryan, *Planning and Leading Bible Study (For Pastors and Lay Teachers)* (Board of Discipleship of the United Methodist Church, 1973) — This book is presented as a resource to help enrich our understanding of the Bible and to suggest some ways of planning, organising, and leading Bible study groups.

Lyman Coleman, Serendipity Series (Word Books).

Titles include: — *Rap*
Groups in action
Serendipity
Coffee House Itch
Discovery
Beginnings
Celebration
Frog Kissing
Breaking Free
Man Alive
Acts Alive

A highly recommended series of books for youth and adult study. Each offers a variety of study approaches and opens up personal and group growth through Bible study.

CHRISTIANITY

J. N. Anderson, *Christianity and Comparative Religion* (I.V.P., 1971).

Joseph Bayly, *Out of My Mind* (Tyndale) — essays on contemporary Christianity.

H. L. Ellison, *The Household Church* (Paternoster).

Michael Green, *New Life, New Lifestyle* (Hodder, 1973).

Michael Griffiths, *Consistent Christianity* (I.V.P.).

Any books by C. S. Lewis, who was one of the wisest and most loving Christians this century.

Paul E. Little, *Know What You Believe* (Scripture Press, 1970).

Paul E. Little, *Know Why You Believe* (Pyramid, 1973).

I. Howard Marshall, *Christian Beliefs* (I.V.P., 1963).

Frank Nicol, *Christian Beliefs* (Joint Board of Christian Education, 1970 — Christian Life Basic Book).

Fritz Ridenour, *So, What's the Difference* (G/L Publication, Glendale, Calif., 1967). A Biblical comparison of orthodox Christianity with major religions and major cults, written to help Christians better understand their own beliefs.

John R. W. Stott, *Basic Christianity* (I.V.P.).

John R. W. Stott, *Becoming a Christian* (I.V.P.).

John R. W. Stott, *Christ the Controversialist* (I.V.P., 1970).

Dick Williams, *Godthoughts* (Falcon, 1969)

Dick Williams, *Godfacts* (Falcon).

CHRISTIAN RENEWAL

Walter Albritton, *Koinonia Ministries Guidebook* (Tidings, Nashville, Tenn., 1969).

Dietrich Bonhoeffer, *Life Together* (Harper and Row, 1954).

Dietrich Bonhoeffer, *The Cost of Discipleship* (Macmillan, 1967).

Robert Arthur Dow, *Learning Through Encounter* (Judson Press, Valley Forge, 1971). Spontaneity — Trust — Openness — Expectancy are characteristics of the learning method presented in this book to help persons come to a new understanding of themselves and their relationships to other people.

Robert C. Girard, *Brethren, Hang Loose* (Zondervan, 1972). A stimulating book which is changing many parishes.

Walden Howard, *Nine Roads to Renewal.*

Bruce Larson, *Dare to Live Now* (Zondervan, 1965, '72). A guide to wholeness, maturity and integrity.

Bruce Larson, *Setting Men Free* (Zondervan, 1967). Sound help for laymen and ministers who want to bring Christ's renewal into their own lives, and the lives of those around them; actual experiences of people. Chapters deal with arts of living, conversation, communication, gifts of humility, freedom, dialogue, love, fellowship.

Keith Miller, *Habitation of Dragons* (Word Books, 1970).

Keith Miller, *Second Touch* (Word Books, 1967).

Keith Miller, *The Becomers* (Word Books, 1973) — Keith Miller opens up the area of life after becoming a Christian in growing and communicating the gospel to others in the world in which he lives.

Keith Miller, *The Taste of New Wine* (Word Books, 1965) — Keith Miller shares some guideposts to a new kind of honesty with yourself and God.

Keith Miller and Bruce Larson, *The Edge of Adventure — An Experiment in Faith* (Word Books, 1974) — Bruce Larson and Keith Miller share their personal experiences in their learning about God and learning to be totally committed to Him. A challenge to our own personal commitment to God. Cassettes are available in a Small Group kit which includes this book and participants' books.

Keith Miller and Bruce Larson, *Living the Adventure* (Word Books, 1976). Deals with issues confronting every person seeking to live an authentic Christian lifestyle. Also available in Small Group kit as 13 week study course. Includes 3 cassettes, Leader's Guide and Response manual.

Danny E. Morris, *The Life That Really Matters* (Wanted 10 Brave Christians), (Spiritual Life Publishers) — The textbook for the 10 Brave Christians Small Group Movement.

Elizabeth O'Connor, *Our Many Selves — A Handbook for Self-Discovery* (Harper & Row, 1971) — From individual and group experiences, Elizabeth O'Connor helps the reader understand his or her own life and evolve a programme of continuing personal growth. From judgment to Empathy and Creative Suffering are discussed.

John Powell, S. J., *why am i afraid to tell you who i am?* (Argus, 1969).

Robert A. Raines, *New Life in the Church* (Harper and Row, N.Y. and Evanston, 1961). Topics covered include conversion, growth of the personal Christian life, koinonia groups, expansion of these groups into the church, and the emergence of the lay ministry and the recovery of mission.

Robert A. Raines, *Reshaping the Christian Life*.

Lawrence O. Richards, *A New Face for the Church* (Zondervan, 1970) — Focusses on the truly basic issues facing Christ's Church today. Divided into four sections dealing with 1) areas of concern, 2) the true nature of the Church as revealed in Scripture, 3) directions to reconstruct local church life, 4) a completely speculative look at the church's "new face".

Rosalind Rinker, *The Open Heart, and Adventure in Discovering the Love of God* (Zondervan, 1969) — For personal or group use on step by step Christian journey.

Samuel M. Shoemaker, *How to Become a Christian* (Word Books, 1973).

Samuel M. Shoemaker, *By the Power of God*.

Samuel M. Shoemaker, *The Experiment of Faith*.

Samuel M. Shoemaker, *Revive Thy Church, Beginning With Me*.

Elton Trueblood, *The Common Ventures of Life* (Words Books, 1975).

Elton Trueblood, *The Company of the Committed* (Harper and Row, 1961).

Elton Trueblood, *The Incendiary Fellowship* (Harper and Row, 1967).

FILMSTRIPS

Check with the Christian Education Department of your denomination for filmstrips, and cassette tapes.

Catalogues available from: C.M.S. Church Supplies, 93 Bathurst Street, Sydney, Scripture Union, each State Australian Religious Film Society, Lutheran Book Shop, Adelaide, and from Challenge Films.

Usually filmstrips are not loaned but purchased. Average price is about $5, with scripts. They cover a wide range of subjects including drug abuse, ecology, youth, sex educaton, parables from nature, evangelism, communication, missionary and biblical topics and Christian beliefs.

JOURNALS

Faith/At/Work — (American). Very highly recommended as a relevant, helpful journal for Christian faith and practice. Subscription $US10.00 each year. Apply:

Faith/At/Work Magazine, Box 1790,
Waco, Texas, 76703. U.S.A.

GROUPS — CHRISTIAN SMALL GROUPS

John L. Casteel (ed.) *Spiritual Renewal Through Personal Groups* (Association Press, New York, 1957) — Valuable insights drawn from a variety of people and places on small groups. Particularly useful contribution by J. W. Meister on prayer groups.

John L. Casteel (ed.) *The Creative Role of Interpersonal Groups in the Church Today* (Associated Press, New York, 1968) — Contributors explain how interpersonal groups in the church can reinforce social action, personality, growth, ability to listen, communication skills, leadership development, religious education and other aspects of individual and corporate life in every church.

Lyman Coleman, *Groups in Action* (Word, Serendipity Series).

Paul F. Douglass, *The Group Workshop Way in the Church* (Association Press, New York, 1956). For those who want to get people to: work more effectively in their church, understand their individual roles in the church, develop stronger leadership in their church. Rich in practical help.

Robert C. Girard, *Brethren, Hang Loose* (Zondervan, 1972). A stimulating book which is changing many parishes.

John Hendrix (ed.) *On Becoming a Group* (Broadman, Nashville, 1969). This symposium provides a non-technical approach to group dynamics within a specifically Biblical frame of reference.

Walden Howard, *Nine Roads to Renewal* (Word, 1967).

Reuel L. Howe, *Herein is Love* (Judson Press, Valley Forge, 1961). Although not technically a book on small groups, this little volume presents one of the best attempts at developing a theology for small groups.

John Kleinig, *The Group — Its Nature and Role* (Anzea Publishers, Sydney, 1974). This book explores the value of small groups in the church.

Margaret E. Kuhn, *You Can't Be Human Alone* (The Seabury Press, 1956). This book is designed to guide any group in the church in seeking to define its purpose, and work towards its objectives, or solve specific problems.

Bruce Larson, *No Longer Strangers* (Word Books, 1971).

Robert C. Leslie, *"Group Experience and Communication in Interpersonal Relations", Religious Education,* L. (March-April, 1955), 106-110 and reprinted in *Journal of Pastoral Care,* XI (Summer 1957), 65-72. Describes and discusses what is involved in making significant communication possible in a group situation.

Robert C. Leslie, *Sharing Groups in the Church: An Invitation to Involvement* (Abingdon Press, 1970-1971) — Guidelines, case studies, and examples for the development and activity of sharing groups. Discusses leadership of groups.

Robert C. Leslie, *Small Groups in the Church: A Bibliography* (Available from Robert C. Leslie, Pacific School of Religion, Graduate Theological Union, Berkley, California 94709, U.S. $1.00).

Sara Little, *Learning Together in the Christian Fellowship* (John Knox Press, Richmond, Va., 1956) — Challenging, yet practical volume on methods of group study; emphasis on Bible study. "Group dynamics" becomes more than an elusive phrase. A sound, widely used textbook for training leaders.

Harold D. Minor (ed.), *Creative Procedures for Adults Groups* (Abingdon Press, 1968). The book is a response to the need of exciting new approaches to adult Christian education. The need calls for guidance in procedures — experienced teachers here describe procedures that can stimulate thought and draw on the experience of the whole group.

Harold D. Minor (ed.), *Techniques and Resources for Guiding Adult Groups* (Abingdon Press, 1968, 1972). The book deals with group life, guiding a study group, ways of learning, resources for learning. Under these four headings are many specific methods and resources, a wealth of information and ideas for anyone seeking guidance in establishing effective adult groups.

Clyde H. Reid, *Groups Alive — Church Alive* (Harper, New York, 1969). A basic handbook, drawing on solid resource, that includes specific reference to human potential groups.

Lawrence O. Richards, *69 Ways to Start a Study Group and Keep it Growing* (Zondervan, Mich., 1973). 69 ways to get going with an effective study group, with five goals in mind: identification with members, strive for affirmation, exploration of scripture, concentration on Christ as the centre of the group, adoration and worship of

God made an exciting experience. A gold mine of resources.

Samuel M. Shoemaker, *With the Holy Spirit and with Fire* (Harper and Row, New York and Evanston, 1960). The author describes what groups of Christians can do when they make themselves channels of the Holy Spirit to influence family life, business, the parish church and ultimately the world.

Michael Skinner, *House Groups* (Epworth Press and SPCK, 1969). A practical book which seeks to show how house groups can help lead to renewal in the local church.

PERSONAL DEVELOPMENT (For individuals or for use by groups)

Earl Jabay, *The God Players* (Zondervan). "How Not To Run Your Life". A transformed psychologist tells how to leave the kingdom of self and go into the kingdom of God. For group study.

Keith Miller, *Taste of New Wine* and *Second Touch* (Word). Books widely used in renewal groups telling of Miller's own spiritual pilgrimage.

Cecil G. Osborne, *The Art of Understanding Yourself* (Zondervan). Fine blending of spiritual and psychological insights.

John Powell, *why am i afraid to love?*, *why am i afraid to tell you who i am?** (Argus Communications Co., 1967). Both of these books offer valuable bases for discussion. *A filmstrip has been made of this book.

John O. Stevens, *Awareness: exploring, experimenting, experiencing* (Real People Press, Box F Moab, Utah 84532, 1971). This book leads you through more than a hundred experiments of discovering your awareness of yourself, your surroundings and your interaction with others.

Dr. Paul Tournier, *The Meaning of Persons.* Worthy of reading and group study. Helpful thinking on "Who Am I?"

Dr. Elton Trueblood, *The Incendiary Fellowship* (Harper & Row). Worthy of study by seeking and committed Christians — or skeptics.

PRAYER

William Barclay, *The Plain Man Looks at The Lord's Prayer* (Collins Fontana Books, 1964). An in-depth study of the Lord's Prayer from the time it emerged to today as a pattern for our prayers.

William Barclay, *Prayers for Young People* (Fontana, 1966).

Herbert F. Brokering, *Surprise Me, Jesus* (Augsburg, 1973).

Betsy Caprio, *Experiments in Prayer* (Ave Maria Press, 1973). This book is aimed at the teacher who is dealing with high school students in a scripture class. All are based on classroom experience. Some of the suggestions may seem a little fanciful and 'way out', but it is well worth searching for ideas.

Maxie Dunnam, *The Workbook of Living Prayer* (The Upper Room, 1974). The book was written to help people learn to practice prayer in a simple, practical way.

Sam Emerick, *Manual for Prayer Groups* (The Institute for Lay Renewal).

E. S. P. Jones, *Worship and Wonder* (Gilliard, 1971).

Ben Johnson, *Learning to Pray* (The Institute for Lay Renewal).

C. S. Lewis, *Letters to Malcolm* (Fontana, 1966).

Thomas Merton, *Contemplative Prayer* (Image Books, 1969) — written by a monk . . . the fruit of decades of study and experience. A practical, non-academic and deeply moving essay on the very nature of prayer.

Thomas Merton, *Seeds of Contemplation* (Clarke, 1972).

Eliabeth O'Connor, *Eighth Day of Creation* (Word, 1971).

Elizabeth O'Connor, *Search for Silence* (Word, 1972).

Cecil G. Osborne, *Prayer and You* (Word, 1975).

J. J. Packer, *Prayer Can Change Your Life.*

William R. Parker and Elaine St. Johns, *Prayer Can Change Your Life* (Yokefellow). Text book of the Yokefellow growth groups.

Rosalind Rinker, *Communicating Love Through Prayer* (Zondervan, 1966).

Rosalind Rinker, *Prayer, — Conversing With God* (Zondervan, 1973).

Rosalind Rinker, *Teaching Conversational Prayer.*

Rosalind Rinker, *Praying Together* (Zondervan, 1968) — A guide to learning to pray in a personal, meaningful way, illustrated with actual cases and examples.

Harold Rogers, *Learning to Listen, Lord* (Word).

W. E. Sangster, *Teach Us to Pray* (The Epworth Press, 1951) — Sangster's concern has been to help beginners with the practice of prayer.

Charlie W. Shedd, *How to Develop a Praying Church* (Abingdon Press, 1964). How the church can become a "Praying church" where each member is prayed for daily by someone and is an example of what the local church can become and how it can continue to grow in experience.

Charlie W. Shedd, *The Exciting Church: Where People Really Pray* (Word Books, Waco, Texas, 1974) — About a caring experiment in a small church. Shedd tells of a practical plan for any church, and answers questions frequently asked about prayer.

Helen Smith Shoemaker, *Schools of Prayer for Leaders and Learners.* A book that will encourage clergy and lay persons throughout the church to experiment bravely and creatively in presenting prayer as well as praying with others.

Helen Smith Shoemaker, *Prayer and Evangelism* (Word, 1974).

S. F. Winward, *Teach Yourself to Pray* (Hodder, 1965).

Anne S. Townsend, *Prayer Without Pretending* (Anzea).

FILMS

Religious films are available for hire from **The Australian Religious Film Society,** 162 Russell Street, Melbourne, 3000 and Cnr. Blenheim Road and Warwick Street, North Ryde, 2113. The Society also has agents in Brisbane, Darwin and Perth. A group can obtain discounts on rentals by joining the society. Film hire prices range from $3.25 to $30. Both Gospel Film Ministry and NAVA Pty. Ltd. (for Insight Films) have offices in State capitals.

FACTS AND FAITH FILMS are distributors of the well-known **Moody Institute of Science Films.** "Sermons From Science" series: 28 minutes, colour, 16mm, sound films of scientific content with Christian application. Latest releases: *Where the Waters Run, In the Beginning.*

CHALLENGE FILMS (a division of Fact and Faith Films) are distributors of Billy Graham dramatic and documentary films, C.E.T.V. productions and those of several other overseas producers. World distributors for *Jungle Doctor* audio visuals. Suppliers of projection equipment, screens, etc.

Libraries located at:— SYDNEY: 400 Kent Street; BRIS-BANE: 426 Ann Street; MELBOURNE: 2A Waltham Street; ADELAIDE: 350 King William Street; PERTH: Second Floor, Bible House, 167 St. George's Terrace; PORT MORESBY: P.O. Box 5536.

Other sources of religious films are Gospel-In-Film Service, 559b Elizabeth Street, Sydney; British and Foreign Bible Society offices; Australian Council of Churches offices; denominational mission boards.

In Adelaide, films may be hired from: Lutheran Book Shop, 110 Gawler Place, Adelaide, 5000 (G.P.O. Box 13681, Adelaide 5001) and Churches of Christ Centre, 104 Gore Street, Adelaide, 5000.

Good quality films can also be hired by film clubs at a reasonable rate. If this interests your fellowship group it would be worthwhile registering as a film club and offering a regular film night in your suburb or town for youth as both a service and a means of outreach. Most of the big film distributors offer hire services, but you will need to check carefully that 16mm prints are available. Lists are obtainable from:

M.G.M., 288 Queen Street, Melbourne, 3000;
Quality Films, Room 5, 2nd Floor, 405-411 Sussex Street, Sydney, N.S.W. 2000.
Australasian Film Hire (Roadshow Distributors) in each State.

The Joint Board of Christian Education has published *Films for Youth Programmes,* which gives outlines of short films, with suggested discussion points. Also *Immediate,* published by Joint Board gives brief comments on current secular films and a discussion guide.

Films can also be borrowed from banks (Public Relations Departments), oil companies and other big institutions, from the Australian Government (State Film Libraries) and from consulates and embassies of foreign countries represented in Australia. The selection of films, filmstrips and slides available from the consulates for Israel is particularly useful for Bible background.

GAMES

Pat Baker and Mary-Ruth Marshall, *Using Simulation Games* (Joint Board of Christian Education — Youth Work Guide Series).

Dennis Benson, *Gaming — The fine art of creating simulating/ learning Games for Religious Education* — book plus two 33 1/3 records, (Nashville, Tenn., 1971).

Lewis and Streitfeld, *Growth Games* (Abacus, 1973) — These enjoyable games are fully explained.

CASSETTE PROGRAMMES

The use of cassettes as a substitute for live speakers can be overdone. They are particularly useful for country people, where it may not be possible to have a big-name speaker address the group or fellowship. Many cassette recorders are not suitable for use in large meeting halls or churches because they have insufficient amplification.

It may be possible for you to interview a resource person or ask him to speak on a given subject for your group.

There are a number of cassette libraries in the cities with a wide range of subject matter available.

Keith Miller and Bruce Larson, *The Edge of Adventure* — A thirteen week programme which provides personal growing as the adventure unfolds. Their Claim — "if you don't change in the thirteen weeks, then you can say there is no God" — but time and again the group members have changed as the adventure proceeds. Very highly recommended.

Fifty Days to Pentecost and *Come, Follow Me* — Both first rate for Church life and work. Increases commitment and makes for renewal. Recommended and produced by the Institute for Lay Renewal.

CREATIVE RESOURCES LIBRARY

A dynamic new series of cassette tape learning materials recorded by outstanding Christian leaders such as: *Keith Miller, Victor E. Frankl, Bruce Larson, Helmut Thielicke, William Barclay, Cecil Osborne, Elton Trueblood.*

The programmes are designed for use in small groups, conferences, seminars and retreats, and include study guide and response sheets. A catalogue is available from:

Gospel Film Ministry,
18-26 Canterbury Road,
Heathmont, Vic. 3135.

John Mallison is well known for the significant role he plays in the small group movement throughout Australia.

He is in great demand as a lecturer, consultant and trainer in many fields of church renewal, particularly the role small groups are playing in bringing new life to the Church.

He draws upon a varied and wide experience. For 17 years he was a parish minister in rural, industrial and developing suburban areas. He soon became recognized for his innovative work in the broad spectrum of parish ministry. A healthy balance between education, evangelism and social concern has been characteristic of his ministry.

This extensive practical experience, combined with 14 years of experimenting with a variety of small groups for youth and adults in different parish situations gives a ring of authenticity and credibility to his leadership in the Small Group movement.

Two overseas visits, during which he observed a variety of small groups in local churches and participated in numerous training experiences in twelve countries further enriches his contribution to the Australian scene.

At present he is Associate General Secretary of the Board of Education of the Uniting Church in New South Wales. His Small Groups Leadership Training courses and retreats throughout Australia have attracted hundreds of people from all Christian denominations. The N.S.W. State Government, secular youth bodies and other church organizations have also engaged him to conduct learning experiences in Small Group work. He has also conducted this training for the church in India and Melanesia.

He is the author of *How to Commence Christian Cells in the Local Church* (1964), *Lay Witness Teams* (1972), *Youth Outreach and Evangelism* (1975), *How to Communicate Your Faith* (1975) and *Christian Lifestyle Discovery Through Small Groups* (1977).

He says his most significant small group comprises his wife, June, and family of four boys and a girl.